Rûnarmâl II
Essays Out of Time

Stephen Edred Flowers

Copyright © 2014
by LODESTAR

All rights reserved. No part of this book, either in part or in whole, may be reproduced, transmitted or utilized in any form or by any means electronic, photographic or mechanical, including photocopying, recording, or by any information storage and retrieval system, without the permission in writing from the Publisher, except for brief quotations embodied in literary articles and reviews.

For permissions, or for the serialization, condensation, or for adaptation write the Publisher at the address below.

Published by
LODESTAR
P.O. Box 16
Bastrop, Texas 78602

www.seekthemystery.com

Contents

The Story of Rûnarmâl II..iv
I. Tradition...1
II. Traditional Esotericism...9
III. Application of Traditional Esotericism 17
IV. Traditional Rune Magic 25
V. The Utility of Objective Traditions............................ 33
VI. Two Forms of Immortality....................................... 39
VII. Two Forms of Reincarnation................................... 47
VIII. Right Hand Path and Left Hand Path
　　as C*operative* Systems 53
IX. Antinomianism? 57

The Story of Rûnarmâl II

The present book has had a curious story as to its generation. It was born of Need and has languished in the doldrums of despair, only to emerge on the eve a new dawn.

In the dark days of 2010, Rûna-Raven was in great need of funds to keep things going. In May of that year I turned to a trusted friend to help produce an audio product of recorded talks to jump-start things. This, like every other project undertaken at that time, was sabotaged. The product never saw the light of day. In the end the talks themselves have been scrapped in favor of written versions of the contents. The original texts for these works began as transcripts of the spoken talks. For this reason the writing found in these texts may be somewhat unusual in their rhetorical style. It must be remembered that they started off as extemporaneous spoken words and evolved into written texts. Their original orality can be seen to shine through frequently.

I have not undertaken to alter the contents of the texts in any radical way. They are simply clarifications of the ideas originally presented in the original talks. In editing them this year I discovered that some of the ideas that were to take shape in 2013 were clearly emerging at the time the talks were first given. The ideas I refer to here are essentially those of the Mazdan *insight*, or the Indo-European spirituality of the Good Religion. In the editing process I have resisted the temptation to expand on the contents in a more overt way to express the Mazdan message more clearly. In essence I would request that the reader bear in mind that the Mazdan message is the same message I have been trying to get across for many years— expressed in a more universal form. It can now be seen that the destruction of operations that occurred in 2011 was necessary to awaken the Mazdan insight. Destruction is not good in itself, but it can stimulate the good as a reaction to the effects of that destruction.

After languishing for three and a half years the contents of *Rúnarmál II* are finally emerging. Its emergence is a sign of the renewal of operations in a radically new form. May the lessons learned from fighting Destruction and Witlessness be the basis for a new blossoming in the garden of the mysteries.

Edred
Woodharrow
Midsummer 2014

I
Tradition

Much is heard today, in certain circles, about the word "Tradition." It is used by Christians as well as by esotericists such as the followers of Julius Evola for example; and when we use the term we are using it more, of course, in the sense of Evola than the Christian way of using it. However our use is also more tinged, with the ordinary definition of tradition, and so it requires some refinement in order for everyone to be able to understand precisely what is meant when — for example — we use the term within the Runic Tradition.

When the Christian uses the term it is rather a travesty in my mind, in the sense that organized Christianity actually represents a destruction of tradition. If we look at the original intent of Christianity we soon realize that it could have not been very interested in actually producing a Tradition in the sense that every generation of Christians, since the beginning, have believed that they were living in the *end of time* and that the world would come to an end. Therefore the traditional elements within Christianity itself are in fact not Christian in origin, but reflections of non- or pre-Christian features. The value of tradition in the Church is something which was inherited from pre-Christian, Indo-European, ideas rather than from truly Christian, apocalyptical ideas which truly run counter to tradition in the sense of carrying on a multi-generational tradition which would — in their mythology — be senseless and useless. The world is ending in this generation, why build a structure for the perpetuation of things into the future?

What is usually understood by the average person when they hear the term "tradition" is perhaps something akin to the stodgy repetition of past forms, a kind of conformism to external formality or pomp and circumstance. But we do not really intend to imply that aspect in our use of the word "tradition," even though at its worst, that is perhaps what tradition is: a repetition of set forms over time. But that is tradition at its outermost, virtually meaningless, level: the stodgy repetition of past forms, in an unthinking manner, while not *using* the forms that are being handed down from generation to generation, or person to person, for their intended purpose, but rather simply repeating them mindlessly.

Even in this worst form of tradition we must realize that there is also great potential value. This is because if things are repeated, handed down in a form, even in a mindless way, there was perhaps originally something encoded there which was full of intent and meaning. But these forms can lose their meanings for various reasons. Either the forms were forbidden to have meaning, so people could carry on the tradition but only if it was considered to be meaningless. For example, the use of a tree at the Yule-Tide in Christianity or in a Christian culture. This is permitted to carry itself onward, but only if the broad mass of people don't understand and fully comprehend what that form of behavior originally meant and what its true origins are. If these were broadly known the practice would probably be forbidden and would then be something that would eventually be eradicated over time. Thus the very apparent meaninglessness and rote repetition of behavior allows it to survive over time and allows the meaningful tradition encoded in the forms to be revivified at a later time. Whereas if it had remained in its constantly original, meaningful form it would have been much more vulnerable to suppression by greater cultural powers at certain stages in history. Apparent meaninglessness is the cover under which meaning-laden forms survive.

But there are also those who are enamored with Tradition for its own sake. Just because something is traditional and just because something has been handed down in some way over time, it gains a certain value to certain people; and these people are — or can be — quickly lead astray. If an idea or an institution has been handed down for centuries in an unbroken chain, then it becomes an end in itself for them they come to believe that it is inherently *good*.

Why is it good?

Because It is traditional.

Just because something has been handed down for hundreds of years it acquires the quality of goodness. It is extremely wrong to think that way. For example, the practice of the abuse of children or the abuse of spouses is often also handed down — more often than not — from generation to generation. What was done to that person when they were young is then repeated by that person to someone else, that is also a tradition. How much worse could it get?

It could get worse, and it has. We find these patterns in Christianity, or Islam. These are actually institutional forms of abuse and just because they are traditional, and have been handed down for hundreds of years, does not recommend itself as being something which is necessarily good. Simply and directly stated: there are good traditions and there are bad traditions. Good traditions are ones that express in an outward way, the inner and eternal values — good values — of a body of people. That could be a tribe, a nation, an organization, such as an Order, or a "church" if you will, an assembly of people, a guild, a gathering of people who become members of something and carry on a way of doing things and certain beliefs about themselves. These things are always useful to them and make them healthier, better, smarter, more reasonable, more insightful, and bonds them more steadfastly to one another.

I am not saying that, for example, Christianity or Islam completely *lack* these things. However, nine times out ten or five times out of ten any good aspects contained within these bad traditions are actually not things inherent to them, but things which they inevitably had to absorb from the preceding culture in order to: 1) be accepted by the people they were trying to convert and 2) because they just work well. For example, after Christianity was installed and was established to a certain extent in much of Europe — in the southern and western parts at least — why did the Pope say in the year 800, "Well we have got a church but we don't have an Emperor, we don't have a general. We need, as "Romans" we need, to have an Emperor. This is remarkable because after all they were so audacious as to say that they were a continuation of the very institution which has *supposedly* suppressed them. The Roman Catholic Church always saw itself as a continuation of the Roman Empire, as it had subverted the institutions of the Empire from within and wanted to retain the "brand name" of *Roman* for the prestige (power) it granted. The Pope wanted a new empire— *Holy Roman Empire*. So he created a new Emperor in the year 800 in the form of Charlemagne, the King of the Franks.

So here we see a carrying forward of old ideas, sometimes foreign to, and even antithetical or antagonistic to, the group in question — in this case the Christians. These ideas will be absorbed and used, becoming part of their tradition, if it is practical, if it is useful to them. And so here we see an example of the preceding culture actually being transparently absorbed. That is just one great example that is so obvious that most people miss it. But there are thousands of other examples that can be discovered in history.

In the idea of Tradition itself there are basically two different ideas at work, which coalesce into one which constitutes the entire idea of Tradition itself. Both ideas have to be present before one can say a tradition truly exists. One is a static/transcendent *idea*. To be *static* means that a thing *stands* as is, it is set, it is an unchanging idea. This is rather like a Platonic idea, that is, things such as justice or truth or beauty etc., as ideas or forms, are eternal. As we observe phenomena in our environments we can deduce these things if we gain insight into the hidden reality beyond appearances.

When we look at a tradition there are certain things which are static, or unchanging, which history or institutions or the people involved do not disturb.

Sometimes even those people carrying on the tradition corrupt or misuse it, or do not carry it out, or mask it, change it, even try to obscure the reality of the nature of the transcendent idea which the tradition is charged with carrying on. Even if all this is done, it does not negate the fact that there was, and is, that thing in existence which was, is, and should be their charge to carry on.

The second part of the idea is a *dynamic* and immanent idea. People have to hold these elements, have to understand them, have to be conscious and aware of them. Then they have to pass them one from one person to the next, and therefore from one generation to the next over time through the course of history. The former idea, the *static* one, is completely *free of history*. It has no history. It just simply exists. It is what it always has been and will be what it is now, for always. This aspect is an important part of the idea of Tradition. It should be said that this is the part of Tradition which Evola most emphasized. But without the dynamic element the static idea remains almost impotent in history. The static or transcendent element is pure Quality. It represents the state of the art, the *state* — static state. This is another way of saying that it is a *state of being*. This is not subject to corruption, its reception and transmission can be corrupted but the thing itself is not subject to corruption. In this it is akin to the element of gold. But in history, when actual people get involved in learning about this thing — whatever it is — and absorbing it, understanding it, there can be flaws in the transmission. There can be flaws in the way the idea is transmitted from person to person, and hence from generation to generation to generation. It is necessary for there to be an element of control in this process. In other words, the human beings involved must make it a significant part of what it is that they are doing to preserve the quality of the transmission from one person to the next, from one generation to the next. The word tradition comes from a Latin word *traditio* which basically means "to inherit" or "to pass on" something. For example, property is inherited from one generation to the next, hence a *traditio* has taken place. This is what the term originally denoted more than anything else. But by the same token ideas or institutions can also be handed down. The danger is that the process can become empty of the higher (static) element or core idea which is the real home of the Tradition. The higher idea is rendered completely invisible and completely cutoff from real live human beings— and it is only with contact with real live human beings who learn it and teach it and hand it on, that the Tradition can be made complete.

Both concepts the *static* and the *dynamic* traditions are fundamental parts of *one whole thing* which is called *The Tradition* or Tradition. One of these things cannot really exist without the other, cannot exist in any real way without the other. The transcendental part, which is what ensures the immortality of the tradition is essential; the immanent part is what gives tradition its living experience.

As mentioned earlier, this transcendental part is often unquestioned at times and passed along as an empty form from person to person, generation to generation. It can be said that when we look at great traditions we see that they are only occasionally revivified by insight, by real spiritual enlightenment. When this happens among certain groups of individuals some of the members of these groups open themselves to a greater awareness. But regardless of when or if this happens, the outer form of the tradition carries on, so that we see the tradition will carry on either with knowledge or in the dark.

And without this carrying forth of things followed by periods of individual and small group insight and awakening which the tradition makes available, the tradition will become lost. This is why it is valuable to hand things on, even if we do not fully understand certain things anymore. It is also often the case if people do not understand something that they will, change the form into something which they think they understand. This process is not limited to things like the Runic tradition or Ásatrú or the ancient Germanic traditions or whatever other philosophical school that comes to mind. Rather this process is found in *any and all things human*. This is because human beings are cultural creatures. If we did not have tradition we would be no better than some kind of ape out in the fields or in the trees somewhere. If tradition was absent we would have nothing. Everything we have is the result of something involving a process wherein someone at some point had *insight*, learned something, and then handed it on to someone else and they made it better and handed it on to the next generation which perfected it. This does not work in the world of ideas, art, politics, etc. This only works in the physical realm of technology, and so on. Let us say one man discovered the use of the lever, a physical principle of engineering. The principle of leverage exists in the static/transcendent world, but until someone learns of it, uses it and then passes it on, it remains purely "theoretical." Once it is applied and passed on from one person to another, then it starts to become a tradition which form part of what could be called a school of engineering. But only with these kinds of things, technological things, do human beings reap the rewards of centuries and millennia of progressive tradition. Such transmissions are straightforward in technology, but in the spiritual real or the realm of personal development or initiation, such linear development is impossible.

Now let us return to the point where I said people will insert things, things already known to them, when they are confronted with things they do not understand. An example of this occurs in the transmission of texts in the Middle Ages. For the most part in the Middle Ages texts were transmitted over time by being copied and recopied in *scriptoria* in monasteries. The monks would write out a text verbatim, then perhaps several hundred years later the text would have to be recopied, or else the paper or parchment would deteriorate and the text would be lost. But over this time period the language and even cultural context of the text might have changed somewhat. So a monk would be copying along and he would come to a point where he would think: "I don't understand what I'm writing anymore, I don't understand this text anymore, the grammar of it is not making sense to me," or "the story itself isn't making sense to me."

So what does someone take it upon themselves sometimes to do?

Well he would try to "fix it." That is, he would insert what he thinks *ought* to be there to make sense out of it. In the history of textual transmission this is called corruption. By this process texts are intentionally, or unintentionally corrupted.

Because they might not have known how the story was supposed to go anymore, they might put things into a story that did not belong there. The narrative became unintelligible to them at some point in time so they changed it and thereby corrupted it for the next generation who will now not have the original text before them. It will be a corrupt version of the text and the next generation of copyists might add even more corruption. Sometimes these corruptions are committed intentionally. The Irish monks, for example, would intentionally tamper with the texts of Old Irish Sagas because of their pagan content. They would either leave things out, or alter the text because they understood all too well that a given passage was going to teach something about pagan theology or philosophy or whatever, and they had no desire to keep these refinements alive. So they either left it out or changed a little bit, but sometimes as a result of this tampering the overall story makes less sense. Therefore these stories are sometimes confusing to modern readers because pivotal motivations or other things have been left out of those particular sagas.

All this merely illustrates with real historical examples how the historical tradition can be corrupted. This type of corruption generally does not occur with *oral* traditions, such as the transmission of the *Rig Veda* over time. The reason for this is that the transmission takes place under the strict supervision of ones who know the uncorrupted "text." It is the *temporal gap* in awareness that leads to corruption.

When we look at examples of the static tradition in the context of the things we are especially interested in, we see that *Rûna*, the principle of Mystery, is a static part of the tradition. It exists. Principles of philosophy, the Virtues for example *exist*. They are unending. This includes ideas such as: you should work hard, that you should be free, and so on. Freedom, Hard Work, things belonging to the Nine Noble Virtues are things which were good a thousand years ago, are good now, and will always be good. The fact that someone says, "Oh, it's a bad thing to work hard, you should just let somebody take care of you, that's even better!" Or, "What do we need Freedom for, that's just a bother. Making all those choices on a regular basis, whether something is good or bad, or what I should do or what I shouldn't do, that's just too much— heck I'm just gonna watch *American Idol*! That will be a whole lot better life, won't it?"

Well, such attitudes and the people who hold them are just opening the gates of Hel — of Death — and they don't even know it because the laziness and other things which tend to corrupt the soul are always lurking and always waiting like the little worms at the base of

Yggdrasill, gnawing at the right order. This process occurs in your individual being as well as in the cosmos and the purpose of tradition is to fight against that entropy— that destruction or these destructive forces. This is because the Tradition is by definition always constructive, always preserving and constructing and developing— not falling down or rotting. But if we look at certain cultures, such as our own at present, certain aspects of such decay are actually idealized, in this way allowing for the bastardization of the very word "ideal". Static ideas within of tradition, ideas such as *Rûna*, such as the Principles, the Virtues, the forms Truth, Beauty, Justice, things like that, all those things are also examples of static forms.

Then there is the *dynamic* tradition, something which is observable in time and space. This is the Whispering, that is, the *reynandi*. This Whispering is the seeking of Truth, the seeking of right forms, the seeking for that which is hidden, that which is difficult to find, and so on. Furthermore, this involves learning how to make this process work, making people aware of certain things, and then trying to impart this to others, and then reawakening that in history— all this is our particular mission. In essence this is the passing of this information from this generation to the next. All of this constitutes the dynamic part of tradition. So in participating at this present moment — what is actually happening as you read these words — is that we are participating in the dynamic part of the tradition. So it is not merely an abstraction but something which is actually happening at this moment in your life.

II
Traditional Esotericism

This particular topic is the most pivotal talk of this particular *Rûnarmál* series. It is the most groundbreaking, I think, of those which we will have in this particular volume. My own work is something which I see as an exercise in traditional esotericism and with the word "traditional" we have to understand as best we can what was conveyed in the first talk on the idea of tradition in general. Why should we — why should anyone — and more particularly why should I — pursue traditional esotericism?

We should pursue it because it is that which is the highest form of human endeavor. Because it is esoteric it involves the seeking of the the unknown and expanding knowledge, and this expansion of knowledge is the one thing that human beings do which other creatures/entities that we know of cannot do, or do not do. If they were to do it they would also be human. We know this to be the case just by observing ourselves throughout history, or at the present moment for that matter. This endeavor is the highest thing, and to do this thing is our particular and peculiar purpose: to seek knowledge. As we seek knowledge we are inherently doing good because it is our particular purpose as humans to do so. Why traditional then? Why not something else?

Well tradition, as we learned in the first talk, has two parts: the transcendent static form and the dynamic process of transmission. In the first place it is something worth handing on, and by worth we mean it is good, it is something which helps humanity or the individual in becoming better. Now, here we do not want to enter into the particular topic of *progress* in this series, but in general we can say that *progress* is a myth of Modernism. Ultimately it must be said that progress in the way that early Moderns believed in it is not possible. We must conclude that no progress in the kinds of things that are most important is ever made for the whole of mankind. We can create better toys, better weapons, better contraptions, better devices, etc. but as far as the underlying purpose of let's say becoming wise, becoming Initiated, becoming awakened, to say that we have made progress in that kind of field would be tantamount to saying that that Joe Schmo whom I know at the occult bookstore or wherever who claims to be a sage is some twenty five hundred times better than that Buddha guy or that Plato dude ever was. But we do have twenty-five hundred times better weapons than they had in their days.

Agree or disagree with Buddha or Plato but nevertheless are you going to compare them to Joe Schmo? Are you going to say that because a man lived all those hundreds or even thousands of years ago that he is categorically inferior?

If you'd said, "Well what kind of weapons did people twenty five hundred years ago use? And are we going to put our weapons up against them?" Then obviously you're dealing with real progress, real change, fundamental development of gadgetry, yes indeed. Gadgetry is one thing, but are we happier because of it? Are we better off spiritually? Are we more enlightened? Are we wiser? Are we more Initiated as individuals or as groups than such individuals or groups were a thousand years, or two thousand years, ago?

The categorical answer must be: No. We are not. We are generally worse off, by far. Those people were technologically far behind us, but as far as spiritual traditions are concerned we must admit that they were culturally superior. It is not that we don't have these things available to us, its just that those damn little worms have been eating away at certain aspects of our society in such a way that we don't utilize them as a culture. So the answer as to why I pursue esotericism is that I am attempting to make myself and others better. According to *my* opinion, according to Edred?

No.

That would be not traditional. If I had some vision where I said: "I have a great revelation, it's never been had before, I have discovered something new, different, no one's ever discovered it before, no one's ever seen it before, it's the key to the history of mankind and the meaning of human life, and I'm going to reveal it to you even though I just invented it."

If I were you upon hearing such a thing I would run away as quickly as possible But this is not what I am saying. We occasionally hear of such prophets, there was one German philosopher by the name Karl Marx, who said something like this. Some fools still follow his words today and most have been greatly influenced by his ideas— even though these ideas have been disproven categorically in that philosopher's chosen laboratory, that of history. Those ideas, like those of most "original" prophets don't work, there are bad "ideas," and bad ideas never work. But he did claim to have discovered the laws of the human universe, just like someone discovers a principle in nature or something, he discovered what he called the historical dialectic which is really a subjective construct of his with some ties to the tradition of Christianity — for example — and the historical aspects of "God's plan" and so on. But nevertheless, it was just subjective guesswork on his part fed by uninformed reactions and prejudices of his own. This is diametrically opposed to what traditional esotericism is. It is not subjective guesswork fed by uninformed reactions and prejudice in which we come to conclusions before the facts are in, in which we have our conclusion and then attempt to marshal our data to make the conclusion that we want appear plausible. This is what "Christian philosophy" (that is an oxymoron of course) does. It is an oxymoron because philosophy is an open-ended system of inquiry. This is what makes philosophy different from religion as two different things in human endeavor. Both are good, both are necessary, but the two should not be confused. When you say "Christian philosophy" you've categorically confused these two different things. You have a conclusion in the form of Christianity and its dogmas but you're now using philosophical jargon to make it *appear* philosophical when in fact it is not philosophical at all. It is simply a dressing up of a pre-judged conclusion. It is clear that no one is seeking anything unknown here. The "big answer" is already known, people just make it look like they are looking for something when in fact nothing unknown is being sought. "Seekers" are simply being led to your preconceived conclusion which is someone's own subjective construct. Illogical or paradoxical data are referred to as "mysteries." Again this is a misuse of a word.

So conversely traditional esotericism is based on patterns which are *inherited* and which are handed down but the *esoteric* part hinges on that *awakening* which occurs in conjunction with this pursuit, and that is necessarily unique, and manifests itself in the life of the individual. All this happens in a *mysterious* way, individually, and it blossoms — if you will — only under the *right* conditions, at *certain times*. All conditions have to be right for each individual. A teacher can never say to a person: "If you swallow this pill of knowledge you'll *get* it." In fact, to the contrary, there are so many factors at work that this is why *traditional* teaching methods are best. Because they simply cover all bases in a systematic way and then individuals who apply these methods in good faith will then have their own moments of awakening which will be unique to them, but it is found that the fundamental quality of the experiences will be comparable to one another in kind or type.

So why pursue traditional esotericism?

The simple answer is that it is the good and right thing to do.

Therefore the pivotal question arises: What is traditional esotericism?

It is the handing down of qualitative concepts which is geared to individual and group development. It is mysterious, it is discontinuous, and cannot be quantified *per se*. It is more an art than it is a science, although we must apply extreme levels of scientific thought; that is rational knowledge, and so forth, in order to do this thing. It is not just something which we create subjectively: make it look pretty, make it look pleasing to the person or the persons or the time or the age in which we are trying to "sell" this idea and call that traditional esotericism or some sort of system of self-development. Just because it *seems* like it is working doesn't necessarily mean that it is in fact working.

Now, to pursue the actual structure of what it is that I do when I practice traditional esotericism. This is something I believe all schools have done and at different times and in different ways. Here I will try to put them together in a straightforward structure which you will be able to find immediately useful. There are three elements to traditional esotericism. These are structure and pattern, the etymology of ideas, and insight.

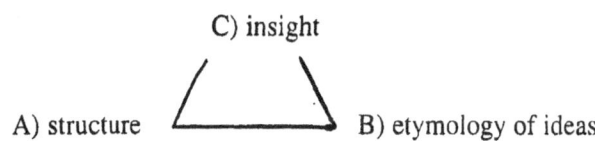

First we have structure or pattern. This shows an inherited pattern, it is stable. Here you will see many corollaries to the first talk. You have a pattern which is before you and let's just say It is the Greek letter Σ. That is your model or pattern and it is to be transmitted from one place to another. We do not question its shape or try to reinterpret it before passing it on. This is the act of accepting, unchanged, a received form. The modern prejudice of mind at once leaps to object to this kind of acceptance of received forms. Some readers probably at once objected: "Oh I don't like to just accept things unchanged." But again if you look back to the first talk you see more context about the utility of accepting, unchanged, a received form. Now the modern prejudice, the modern knee-jerk reaction of mind, at once leaps into wanting to change things to conform to that individual's *present* basic understanding of things. And what happens when this occurs? What happens when you see the Greek letter Sigma Σ and you say, "Oh it looks like an S, sort of, so I'm just gonna change it to an S. It looks better this way so I'm just gonna go ahead and do it. It looks better, I like it better, I understand it better. That other thing looks funny, I don't like it."

This is an uncritical, prejudiced approach. In other words, there is no respect for the idea of accepting in an unchanged way a received form. The feeling for that act, or that process, is corrupted in our present culture. Am I suggesting this just because I'm expressing my own prejudices?

Well, I was born in the Modern Age also and I mostly remain a Modern person despite all my efforts, but I continue struggle against this. On the other hand I see that in certain things ancient and traditional peoples had distinct advantages over us. My first sort of "working" that I performed of a real, more sophisticated type — not just trying to get a girlfriend or get a job or something — but rather something of a higher sort, was one that concluded with the statement:

"The ancient world had great philosophical insight in reality and traditional culture that we now lack. But we have great technology and comforts and all the great things we have. Why can we not combine these to create a more ideal world." I admit that I was only eighteen when I did this working, and if I had been a little older or a bit more educated I might have seen that a lot of smarter, better people than me have had this same idea. But for *me* it was an "original" insight at the time and that was to say: Why do ideas of mythic tradition and technical advancement seem to mutually exclude each other in our society?

Historically the answer lies in the dogmas of the Christian church and other corruptions of its ilk. We lost the cultural capacity to develop in a balanced way and the cult of "monotheosis" (the cultural disease caused by monotheism) forced us to choose between "this" and "that." This is our modern struggle. But why not combine myth and technology? Why not create or encourage the shaping of a culture of the future which unifies these two things?

I suppose I've been working on that problem ever since.

But what happens if certain important things are not accepted as unchanged received forms? What if, even before we think we just go ahead and feel empowered to change something without ever understanding it?

What happens in such a case?

No significant development can possibly take place in that environment because one is constantly just bringing everything down to the level one is on at the present moment, not looking at it as a *mystery* and saying: "Wow, what *is* that thing? I'm just going to copy it down the way it is, look at it the way it is, and try to understand it for what it is."

Rather than saying, "Well it looks kinda like this other thing I already know so I'm just gonna reduce it to what I already know." In this latter case what can I have learned?

Nothing! I have learned nothing! I'm just sitting in the same place I was before, even though a great gift has been bestowed upon me in the shape of this received form, but I didn't accept it unchanged. I had to change it to what I already knew. That is the bread and butter of the occultizoid nincompoop universe, right? Many of them do not like my books. The huge masses don't like them because they tell them things they've never heard before. You'd think an "occult" type person would be looking for the *hidden*, the *unknown*, the *mysterious*— but no. Most do not. People want to read what they already know, or think they know. Books which feed their preconceived notions are the ones they love. It just reinforces that which they already know or already believe. It tells them nothing new, it only tells them what they already know, therefore they like it. It pleases them. It is like a fast-food hamburger.

It is killing them, but nevertheless it is pleasing to them. Other examples of structures are the Fuþark, the texts of Eddic poems, etc.

Then we have the idea of the *etymology of ideas*. This recognizes that under force of this whole process, things do in fact change. The subsequent forms are not the absolute archetypal pattern, but rather they are reflections of the way people have understood this form over time and space. This is analogous to the etymology of a word. For example, let's take a rune-name in its oldest Proto-Germanic form: *fehu*. This becomes Old English *feoh* and that then becomes our modern English word "fee." Now we've gone through three forms of a word thought time, sounds that we can hear a difference in, *fehu, feoh*, fee. This is the same word, the same what is called an "etymon," that is it has the same archetypical root. Additionally, this root is recognizable if you have the key to recognition. If we take the word "fee" and reconstruct *feoh* from that by comparing it across attested English dialects and then among various older Germanic dialects, we arrive at the reconstructed form of *fehu*. Same etymon. They appear to be different words, but there is an unchanged structural seed-pattern which rules the laws of change. This process traces the seed form which goes through history and people over centuries of time. But in each stage there is a *genetic link*, a *contagious link*, between each stage. That is one form actually touched the next one— *fehu* touches *feoh*, *feoh* touches fee.

If one knows the rules and regulations hidden connections can be discovered. Some of the rules at work here are that, for example *fehu* has a short vowel, the *-u* drops and the vowel length is increased a little to compensate for the loss of the final *-u*. This is called "compensatory lengthening" in linguistic jargon. Then in "fee" we have the additional loss of the *-h*, and the vowel becomes even longer.

The lengthening of the vowel sound is a *compensation* for the loss of the subsequent sounds, but this loss leaves behind a pattern, it leaves an audible trace of itself so we know that something is missing. Even before we discovered what was missing in the word "fee" we could have guessed that something was indeed missing because we are familiar with the genetic links between verbal structures in the history of the English language.

Words are similar to ideas, they are analogous to them, and in these genetic links we see that there are also *semantic shifts* in the development of a word. That is *fehu, feoh* and fee are not completely identical in *meaning*. This is also true of ideas, of traditional ideas, or of notions otherwise. For example, in the Indo-European tradition there would just be Indo-Europeanism. Indo-European gods, Indo-European ideas; there wouldn't be Greek and Roman and Celtic and Germanic languages, religions, ideas, concepts. The fact that there are differences between and among the various branches of the Indo-European family tree is testimony to the process of change which occurs under the influence of experience in time and space of real live human beings. The various ethnic traditions are responses, historically and geographically, and in every other way, to differences in human experience. The basic forms are moved through experience in real human life and if the genetic link between ideas is maintained in a healthy way then those higher ideals will feed and guide the health and well-being of the development. If it is broken and opened to corruption, such as that introduced by Christianity, then the transmission is unfocused. Individuals can also alter traditions in unwise ways. We are reminded of Mickey Mouse as the sorcerers apprentice in *Fantasia*. He learns a little secret, pretty soon he has almost destroyed himself. That's the Frankenstein myth, of course — or the Golem myth — a little knowledge misapplied will end up destroying you.

In the world of ideas it seems we are virtually on the eve of destruction as far as what we have done with the world of ideas and the world of culture, in an intellectual or spiritual sense. In this case the etymology of ideas has become corrupted and is increasingly uninformed by higher structures or patterns. So we see that under normal conditions, under the best of conditions, we will have a genealogy of ideas, of semantics. Going back to our established example *fehu* means livestock of some kind, *feoh* means cattle or sometimes even sheep. Then a head of cattle becomes a unit of measure, of monetary value, and thus the semantic door is opened to our present-day understanding of the word "fee." But when people hear the word "fee" today they just see people writing checks or giving money to each other. No livestock comes into people's minds any more when they hear the word "fee." This is because it has semantically shifted. But that key concept of a head of cattle being a unit of measure — historically at a certain moment — that's where you can see the bridge between an animal and a coin.

Although *fehu* meant only livestock *feoh* or Old Norse *fé* could just as easily mean "gold" as anything else, so the transition in meaning, or semantic shift, occurred a long time ago. But you have to be able to explain and see, not just say: "It meant X yesterday but today it means Y," and there's no connection between the two other than the tyrant just says, "What once was X shall now be Y, believe it or die!" This is just force, tyranny, there is no great significance to that. It is just ignorance. That has no place in our way of thinking. Rather there must be discernible *links* between and among all things.

The A and B points of this model always show similarities or linkages, they are concerned with similarities, linkages, analogies, connections, and they form an organic whole— A and B: structure/pattern and etymology of ideas. The C-point in this model is insight, original thought, inspiration— a light goes off. Working along with A and B — structure and pattern and etymology of ideas — suddenly I have an *insight*.

Based on what?

Based on the tradition. These are the patterns that I've been looking at and working with, but then I will get an original insight which connects them in a slightly different way— but only a slight little difference in the way things are looked at can make an enormous amount of difference. Here we have inspiration. Inspiration comes and the "new ideas" occur. "New ideas" can be an oxymoron, I realize. What is really meant is a new *way* of looking at (eternal and timeless) ideas which respond to present needs, to my needs personally at this moment in time in my life, to this culture's needs at this moment in history. This is how the tradition changes or evolves. It will be seen that insight often comes at a critical moment. And these three elements — structure, etymology, and insight — must be present for an individual to work well in this tradition, they must be in some sort of balance among themselves and occur in a dynamic flow. All must be present and a maximum balance of these elements is tantamount to a high level of truth derived from these elements. So as I look back on how I have worked over the years I see that this model represents the structural pattern of how I have worked with esoteric matters over time. Additionally it appears to me that this is how most traditional schools have worked and evolved in the past.

Sometimes I will say, "I'm practicing traditional Runic studies or traditional runology." To this a response may come: "So am I! I have read and studied Ralph Blum! I got this information directly from Ralph Blum. I received these truths from Ralph Blum and his book, and so I'm working a traditional way too."

How can the pseudo-traditionalist be separated from the actual traditionalist? The answer to this question has been the subject of this section of the *Rûnarmâl*. It has made the elements of the traditional approach clear in such a way that texts or teachings based on subjective inventions can be excluded from consideration.

III
Application of Traditional Esotericism

In the last section I wrote about the elements of traditional esotericism, those being structure or pattern, etymology of ideas, and then insight; but now I would like to apply those, or demonstrate them within work that I've done so as to make it as practically understandable as possible. I have tried to give many examples over the years of the application of traditional methods in my works. Whether I wrote about Runes, Ogham characters, Hermetic magic, the Tarot, etc., I always used the method and the approach that I outlined in the second section. Subsequently and concurrently others have begun to be able to do this same thing, and this is the most important thing to convey, that what we are talking about is a *way* of looking at things, and not only *looking* at them (that's only half the story) but rather *applying* these ideas in acts of creativity, of actually using these ideas to move objects in the world, create monuments, works, and actions and to make a difference in the world informed by these elements.

At present in the Lodestar workshop we have people working on things completely different from what we have ever done in the past. An example, just to pick out one example of something someone is actually working on, is that of the ancient Japanese philosophy connected to the syllabary of the Japanese language. The sounds of the this language are encoded in the five vowels and a set of consonant-vowel combinations. The total syllabary comprises some fifty such vowels and consonant vowel combinations. In ancient Japan there developed a belief, and this belief has been carried forth into the contemporary Japanese culture, that these sounds should have power beyond mere arbitrary noise. This is because Japan is still a traditional culture despite all the Elvis impersonators and other strange things that might also emerge there. Japan is a great example of a culture being hyper-modern and being a place where tradition is still absolutely possible to follow without selling one's soul to either extreme. This doctrine of linguistic philosophy is called *kotodama*. This means something like the "spirit of the word"— that is that there is some kind of *power* in sound and that these powers are codified in the Japanese syllabary, and that each syllable has a specific esoteric meaning, etc. This whole area lies outside my field of expertise, and so it must remain a project for others to undertake using the methodology of RÛNA— the Polarian Method. This project is being handled well by others. Will it work, is it working? Of course it will work, because the principles are universal! The things I'm talking about here in *Rûnarmál II* as well as in *Rûnarmál I* are actually universal principles. This universal aspect is addressed more in *Rûnarmál I,* but we need to see things applied in order to understand them more completely. We have to apply them in order to make use of them. They are not the objects of armchair philosophizing but rather they are for practical things. These are the tools of humanity and must be used like a hammer and an anvil.

As an example let's ask what is the structure and pattern in the Runic world?

Obviously the answer is the Fuþark!

There is a structure and pattern inherited over time and space. Twenty four letters divided into three groups. In a certain order characterized by the *pars pro toto* code-word *fuþark*— these being the first six sounds of this system. This grid constitutes its structure or pattern.

Many would-be esotericists of the last quarter century have quickly and easily just started to monkey around with the forms of the Runes, their names, the order of them, happily just saying: "Oh, I'm gonna scramble all these up! Oh yea, I got this new way of looking at 'em! Ha! Just scramble them all up, do 'em in a different order. Do I understand or know anything about the original first order? No, but I don't care. I am expressing my own original genius!"

Well I think in a way their approach suits me fine because they will make no inroads into the actual runic tradition and will remain always on the outside looking in. This chaotic, non-traditional approach often proves popular because it in no way challenges the essence of Modern Man, does not challenge the modern way of thinking. It is this kind of willy-nilly, arbitrary nonsense, where things sort of make sense every once in a while, but where things are never fully coherent, that characterizes Modern American culture. If you create works that mirror this way of thinking you may be effective at making an audience believe you are intelligent or correct. For example, if you are trying to manipulate someone into "buying" what you are "selling" (be that a product, an idea or a political candidate), you're not going to approach a scattered, subjective person whose thought processes don't make sense most of the time, with something coherent and whole. Your audience will tend to be frightened by this and will not respond to you in a positive way. These are merely basic laws of communication. But if the product you are presenting to them, be it art or a book or novel, is also somewhat incoherent and meaningless, but every so often gives off a spark of meaningfulness, will commonly be recognized and responded to. This is also basically a law of communication. But we are not just trying to communicate for the sake of communicating, we are trying to evolve. We are not practicing advertising, we are practicing magic. So we are trying to change the objective universe: maintain those parts of it which are good, develop those parts which are good into better parts, and bring these things together to try to restore something which is right and good. In so doing, and only in so doing do we make war on the destructive and ignorant patterns that often govern parts of ourselves and the world.

So, when we refer to Runic things, we intend to indicate the methods outlined here. We accept the Fuþark system unchanged. I cannot say that I understand the system completely, even to this day I don't understand it completely. Day by day the system becomes clearer with work. More things about this system are constantly being discovered, and in fact the system is probably inexhaustible. But if you do not accept the basic system in an unchanged way, none of its mysteries can be ever be revealed to you. If you don't accept the form unchanged it will simply feedback to you what you already know. And if you're a dumb-ass it will simply teach you to be a dumber-ass. This feedback loop is how much of the mass-media are working today in our culture. But what we are trying to do is something different, we are trying to convey perennial ideas. The first step in doing this is the acceptance of certain structures or patterns in an unchanged way, for example the Fuþark system.

So whatever it is you approach, whatever tradition it is, you look at at it first in this way. I don't care what it is. This does not exclusively refer to esoteric or apparently esoteric traditions.

If you say: "I wanna be a plumber."
Your teacher will tell you: "This is how pipes fit together, son."
Someone might then say, "Oh, I wanna do it some other way."
But the teacher must say: "No! This is the way it is done!"

Now let's just start with the basics and get those things down, and if you wish to become a great innovator later on, and be a Thomas Edison of plumbing, then you can do that, but you must learn the basics first. The first thing that happens is you accept the basic structures and patterns unchanged and unravel their mysteries. If this is an esoteric tradition this task may well take a lifetime, no matter what it is.

Then when we apply the etymology of ideas, we see that all the ideas we have or that we gather together, and things connected with them, have a history of change and transformation. This is the history of ideas. This is what we mean by the etymology, the changing, of ideas. But why "etymology"? This word clearly indicates that the ideas have to be *genetically* linked. This linkage is present both in form and meaning. Thus, for example, when we look at the gods in the Indo-European world we see that the forms of their names seldom survive from one culture to another intact. But forms and functions are easily conveyed. So when a god appears off in the distance in a long cloak with a big wide brimmed hat and some kind of long stick the Greek can recognize Hermes in this image whereas the Germanic man sees Wodan. From the Indo-European perspective this is the same archetype— that of the poet-magician and metacommunicator. It is the same god derived from the same pattern, inherited from the same basic principle, and conveying similar ideas over time to various historical cultures. The same idea or pattern inherited, subjected to cultural and historical permutations, and thus the forms are altered. But they are altered in a systematic way, which allows for their recovery and re-synthesis. No matter how it changes you can still recognize the linkage, you discover the connections, and in discovering these linkages and similarities you are gaining insight, gaining food for your own insight.

Then at a certain moment in the pursuit of these things — in the pursuit of this knowledge, in the learning of these things, and the exercise of the mind within these forms — a sudden flash of insight occurs. This is what, for example, the work of the *Nine Doors of Midgard* and things of that nature are designed to do. Such methods have a long lineage. Plato would suggest that if one wanted to become a philosopher king, if one wanted to gain some kind of enlightenment, a person would have to study mathematics for twenty years and then learn logic and then learn to apply these things to ethics and cosmology. All these things require great discipline, but the ultimate outcome is that the student will gain insight and be able to understand things in an apparently magical way. But does that come without a connection— from just being a Joe Schmo off the street into being a philosopher king, by *hocus pocus*, by just tapping the guy on his head or sprinkling some water on him and then suddenly he has this capacity for insight in any real way?

Of course not.

You may be able to fool him into *believing* he has knowledge, if you want to sell him this thing as an "enlightenment-product." That is the essence of the historical scam called the Church— that spiritual insight, salvation if you will, can be gained in a simple ceremony of some kind which you have to get from an authorized provider who's licensed to provide this service. But the "good news" is that you don't have to work for it, it just happens when you purchase the product. Whereas the ancient and traditional world would say that you have to *work* for it. You have to work at it, you have to be disciplined, you have to develop yourself and then help others, and in teaching you learn even more than what you learned as a student. In this whole process you truly develop yourself.

If you look at the difference between these two approaches you see that one is very self-centered, very selfish. They say: "I just wanna get saved and the rest of y'all just go to hell, I don't care, I'm getting mine from a licensed service provider over here, and then that's it!" Whereas the other says, "You have to work. You have to absorb. It is a whole matter of culture and that involves other people, and that means not just you get better but other people get better. When other people get better the whole society gets better or stays good."

This latter sentiment was very much alive in the ancient pagan world, and was codified in the ancient Mazdan religion derived from Indo-European paganism. More often than not pagans felt that the world was good and that they were trying to hold onto something good, rather than creating something new. So they might say: "This is a good world let's try to preserve it." But when decay sets in, as it inevitably must, we must be able to say: "Things are getting bad we need to restore things, we need to make things better." In a system wherein it is said that people have to work for improvement for which they themselves are responsible, the world will always be improving because there are so many auxiliary benefits from having to work for it rather than just passively, and erroneously, believing that you have something which the service provider has told you that you have but which is really just a bill of goods. The passive approach sets up the individual to accept totalitarianism and tyranny. The traditional approach never lets one forget what the Good is.

These ideas are not merely applicable to esoteric traditions and personal development. They are cultural issues. When people are willing to receive their daily bread from their neighbors' coffers, ripped from the neighbor at the point of the tyrant's sword, they have rendered themselves slaves and slaves cannot be free and cannot develop. Kids who cannot read are given high school diplomas— as the service provider sets up a little rite to certify that Joey has a brain after all.

Culturally this whole world of degradation is the result of the *secularization* of the Christian idea: "I got baptized in the river down there and now I'm a spiritual, enlightened being!"

"How do you know?" the man asks.

"Well the service provider here said it was true, you see? And so that's it and so whatever I think now is what God thinks, because I know what God thinks! It's easy."

Scratch the surface on a person like that and you will find in every case a person who didn't work for it. So when we apply these ideas of traditional esotericism, it involves work. It is characterized by the word *work*. You have to work on discovering the structure and pattern, but that is the easiest part, because this mostly involves accepting what is taught. For example if you are learning a language you don't say why are there four cases and three genders in German? Why can't they do it like we do it?" The students moan and groan because there are three genders and four cases and then they complain: "Why does it have to be that way, I just can't accept it." Well, they don't learn it very well with that kind of attitude, but if you just realize that different languages are in fact *different* it becomes easier. Before progress can be made in learning the patterns of reality must be accepted.

So, the *etymology of ideas*, discovering the connection between and among ideas over time and also your relationship to them is really the crux of the objective part of the work. In doing this work long enough, and diligently enough, moments of insight will come. When those moments come, what are they responding to? What are those insights, what are those sparks of insight illuminating? What will you see if you are working in the dark in this world, meditating and thinking about these forms and exposing yourself only to traditional forms and their permutations and so on? If you remain within a traditional framework and can account for the historical permutations logically or structurally then your results should be useful.

When the spark comes, and the insight comes, you will make connections which are within the structural framework, but which perhaps no one has ever seen before— or perhaps has not seen for a long time. Those will seem to be "original" thoughts or "original" insights and inspiration which result in real knowledge.

If you do not work with archetypal forms and structures your supposed insights will probably not have truth behind them and they will not communicate in a real way. Your vision will not be accurate despite the fact that you may think you are a brilliant genius. But because you were not working with the true forms your great invention is a completely meaningless, and even detrimental — especially to yourself. And so that is why, when we apply traditional esotericism, we apply it to traditional forms, things which have been received. The connections between and among the elements are established and so when insight comes it bears real fruit of actual knowledge and not just something that appears to be true, but which is actually an illusion. This is why I love to see it when people get sparks of insight and see that when they work with traditional forms they bear forth eternal knowledge into the world.

But most of the time most of the communications I have received over the years have not fallen into this happy category.

Rather they have fallen more into the modernistic category of people saying: "I've been working with the "ruins" for a year. Look at my new revelation!" I have one gentleman, he has been writing to me for years and years and he keeps trying to connect the runes to the Tarot. Now, he might have first been inspired by my book *Futhark* and the list of Tarot correspondences in the back of that book. That list was a purely subjective exercise. I say as much in the text where I mention that if you want to work with this idea of Tarot correspondences here are some possible speculative connections. But at the time I wrote this I knew little about the Tarot and certainly nothing about the connection, or possible historical connection, between the runes and Tarot. Subsequently I discovered the work of the early 20th century Swedish scholar, Sigurd Agrell, who worked with this idea in a very insightful way, in the way I'm talking about here. From his work I gained some real information about a connection— of the kind characterized by my formulation of the *etymology of ideas*. Notice that when he made the connection it was based on structural laws, whereas this gentleman, or I myself in the book *Futhark*, just said, "Ok, *Kenaz*, that seems like it has to do with eroticism, so maybe that should be The Lovers of the Tarot." What nonsense! Just making all kinds of willy-nilly subjective connections between and among random elements, unconnected to one another, inorganic kinds of connections, all very arbitrary is no way to seek the truth. That is not the way a tradition works. If you are rediscovering something that is traditional, it will have a great amount of the structure and method which is inherent within the tradition you are working with. This will be present within your discoveries.

An example of this from my own work is the system found in the *Magian Tarok*. It is not my system really, but that of the aforementioned Swedish scholar, Sigurd Agrell. He made a startling discovery about the connection between the Runes and the symbolism of the Tarot. The systems line up when he makes one small change in the Fuþark order (his famous Uþark modification). One small shift is made, keeping everything else in line, and the meanings line up in such a way that it seems obvious there is some kind of connection between the two. Just one little elementary change and everything works, or seems to work, quite in excess of any coincidental explanation. This is an exercise in insight.

Another example is how I discovered the Tree of Life in the Hermetic tradition. There I established a checking mechanism as to how the Greek letters were to be attached to a particular Tree of Life model. I applied this method for attaching the Greek letters to the Tree form in a logical way, which is explained ahead of time. After doing this I discovered that all of the vowels of the Greek alphabet form a continuous chain from the bottom of the Tree to the top of it. This was the confirmation by tradition that the system was correct. This pattern of vowels fits with the idea of the "vowel song," of singing the vowels of the Greek alphabet as a mode of ascending, of causing the soul to ascend, from the Earth to Heaven. Again, if you are proceeding in a traditional way you don't say, "Ok I'm just gonna arbitrarily throw things up there. It just *feels* right to me," that's not the way a tradition would work. You do not need any brilliant insight to splash your preconceived notions on the page. You make it up and then just ask, "Does it look good to you Joe?" And Joe says, "Yea, looks good to me, I think we can sell that! It's so random, and it's so incoherent you know, although you use some symbols there that people might respond to, I think the message as a whole would be very attractive."

No, that is not right.

This is not obtaining real insight based on tradition and that is what we want to do. Now some weisenheimer asks me, "Why do you want to do it?"

The answer is because that is what works as an exercise in development of your mind. And this is where the quest starts— with an exercise of one's own mind. Even if you do nothing else with these ideas and share them with no one else, yet you want to use them for your own self development do you think taking the path of working with traditional elements, learning them, connecting them together, meditating on them, making them part of yourself and the way you think, working with things handed down genuinely in form and fashion from antiquity and then working on them until your own personal insights become living, vivified parts of your consciousness will work? Do you think you are going to develop using that method better than using the alternate method which is: "I'll take what I already know, dress it up in a new aesthetic, and call call myself wise."

I think everyone already knows the answer.

IV
Traditional Rune Magic

This topic is something by which we will further emphasize the ways of working with the traditional methods that I have been outlining. Again these are, as I see them, unfoldments of Runic principles, of hidden principles of things which are not apparent, obvious, or something which is necessarily revealed at all times. Here again we are working with the accepted structure and pattern of the Fuþark, we are working in a *runic idiom* and with the ways in which these principles develop and lay themselves out through a specific mythology, culture, tradition, history, in language, and so forth. By doing this we discover the *etymology of ideas* underlying the external forms. When we are engaged in doing all of that we are involved in a process of revelation. The revelation is not complete until the *insight* comes and at that point a person is ready to work *creatively* with the things which have been learned. Mastery, to some degree or another, has been attained. When the ideas become living realities based upon the deeper principles, not subjective willy-nilly kinds of inventions — arbitrary inventions — then insight is gained into traditional forms.

So when we look at traditional rune magic we see something which runs deeper than the use of a runic symbol for *sorcery*. By sorcery I mean the use magical technology for everyday purposes, e.g. money spells and the like. Someone with little knowledge of runes or runic tradition but who has a really strong talent for sorcery could obtain good results. It is also found that the *belief* that runes are somehow powerful "juju" can help a sorcerer make runes work in a sorcerous way — all this depends on the magical talent of the individual. But that is not the kind of magic we are talking about. These two kinds of magic are intimately connected to each other but sorcery is not our primary aim here.

One of the earliest lessons I learned, or heard, and then only later actually absorbed and learned, was that the magic forms for self-development are superior to critical applications of magic. Critical applications are those based on crises coming in your life. A crisis comes and you apply a sorcerous solution to it. "I don't have a job; I need to do some magic to get a job. I don't have a girlfriend; I need to do some magic to get a girlfriend." Now if you just developed yourself in a way which is coherent, true, good, strong and intelligent all those crisis points would be absorbed into one overriding thing. Then everything else will work out as it should and you won't have to be worrying about those kinds of things and creating spells to get what you want. And those crises will become much fewer in your life, and also when they do come you will tend to take them in stride, no matter how bad they *seem* to be, rather than becoming upset by them. All this comes with individual development. It is also the essence of the *original magic*, that is, that which was practiced and is being practiced by the original magi, the *magavans* of the Mazdan tradition.

So when we look back at ancient rune-magic and observe the way the ancients used runes, a key, pivotal, question has to be asked: Given the nature of RÛNA the idea of the unknown, of the hidden, of the unmanifest, etc., and its eternal value, are the aims of rune magic today exactly the same as they were in ancient times?

The answer to some extent is yes, but there are other needs we have connected with runes. Rune-magic is there to alleviate need — *naudiz* — and that's why this particular rune plays such an important part in the system. Given this, we have to assess what our individual and cultural needs *are*, and it is to this Need which RÛNA responds. This idea or a response to Need is in the tradition of runic magic, and so using them in a traditional way does not necessarily mean the rote repetition of aims and methods of ancient times.

So what is a rune?

We all probably know the answer to this by now, to the extent that it can be known. The word "rune" meant "mystery" in ancient times. The individual runes are derived from *the* Rune. That is, from the secret or the mystery. Each one is an articulation of a part of this greater mystery. The whole system is akin to *a periodic table of the unknown*, the fuþark. So each rune is akin to an element. Tellingly, this is the word the Greeks used to describe their letters (*stoichia* = elements). It is the same exact word they used for the *elements*: fire, air, earth, and water, etc. So there appears to be an Indo-European tradition of using a system of sound keys as something which functions as a periodic table of world elements which transcends matter but also includes the natural world. These are elements of the unknown or elements of spirit rather than of matter only.

So what then is magic?

Magic is an act of will which facilitates a response by the world to that act which is analogous to the desire expressed through the act of will. So here we are clearly describing a form of meta-communication, wherein symbols are used which have an intimate connection with all levels of reality. To put it in the simplest terms which oftentimes are the most insightful: when a message is put into runes it is transliterated into the code of the gods, or of the realm shaped by Wōðanaz, and thus the message feeds our realm of occurring events. The secret code feeds the event horizon from beyond this mundane existence. If we find the code we can insert our desired message into the code. The idea of magic presupposes a unified code between the spiritual and mundane worlds, or the symbolic and natural realms. This unified field theory is common among Indo-European pagans and Zoroastrians, but is denied by Abrahamic systems.

Furthermore there are purely "spoken runes"— the result of conscious awareness of the runes linked to each of the sounds as one speaks. In this way runes are spoken, but when they are inscribed they are symbolically made more potent through the semiotic equivalence of prestige, perfection and permanence. Thus these symbols or signs translate language in a meta-linguistic way into the language of the gods from whom the code was originally received.

On a constant and ongoing basis when the message is sent in this code, it is then inevitably fed back to the sender — either ourselves or into the environment around us — in another code, another "language" — which is the language of *events, occurrences* or *phenomena* rather than symbols.

So symbols are translated into phenomena through the agency of the runes and the Rune. And we have to some extent be the master of each of the components in order to be able to communicate coherently and thus gain the kinds of return communications which we need. Although some people have a talent for making things work on an ongoing basis in an almost scientific way, for most people their magic works best in a "foxhole." By this I mean that when our backs are to a wall, and it feels like it is a matter of life or death, magic generally works most reliably. It is in moments of crisis and high emotional need when magic works best. This is because magic is an *art* not a *science*. One must be inspired to do this extraordinary act; but certain kinds of magic are done on a routine basis, which is mainly what is known as initiatory work. But again this is something that requires thousands of hours of work to get the flow moving and beyond this is is a lifetime of continuing work.

But I would say this about magic also, that magic provides to us what is otherwise unavailable. Historically it is not a method for providing something which otherwise can be done in a more ordinary way. Rather it provides us something which is otherwise impossible— or at least improbable. To the ancients it might have been magic to be able to fly though the air on a magic carpet or something, but we have airplanes for that now. We don't need to fly through the air on a magic carpet. On the other hand certain things in their lives and their world were quite ordinary, but which have now been lost to us and at this juncture it requires magic to recover it.

They would see our world and think we lived in a universe of magic, if we went back to theirs we would think that they too were living in a universe of magic of a different kind. How do they do the things they do, and they would say the same things about us, but we are each lacking something. Both would also see, if they survived long enough, what was lacking in each other. They would discover how empty and shallow we are, and we would discover how lacking they were in those things which provide comfort and enjoyment in life. They were constantly working in one way or another — even their recreation was a necessary time of rest and "recharging" of the life force needed to survive. Each of us would have something valuable. Our ancestors fought long and hard to build the world we live in, but it is in some respects rather like a Frankenstein's monster or a Golem kind of creation on their part, in the sense that in certain areas they they lacked wisdom in how they designed the system. Of course, I sometimes point to Christianity as being the major disruption in the flow of the design, but I get tired of that criticism or *excuse* myself sometimes. Everything is not perfect, their efforts were not perfect, neither are ours, but we strive for the best and we would see in their world there were things which were lacking and they would see the same in our world.

What is important for us now is to understand that which we lack and work on this shortcoming by means of extraordinary methods of the spirit we call "magic."

In traditional rune magic we look at old formulas, real runic formulas, actual runic inscriptions; we analyze them, of course which I've done in my dissertation *Runes and Magic* to a great extent, we look at what the aims and methods of these formulas were we will renew those old formulas and use them again creating new messages in ways analogous to the ways the old messages were shaped. But the genius of the runic tradition in ancient times was its flexibility. When you have the periodic table of reality, a spiritual periodic table such as the Fuþark represents, all nuances of communication are possible in mysterious and magically effective way. So you can literally speak to the event horizon, you can literally write to it and get phenomenal results back in the form of a meta-communication. Therefore new formulas are also possible, but always under the philosophical constraint of objective meaningfulness.

By that I mean it is under the constraint of something analogous to grammar in a natural language. If you were just a child, untrained in communication in the language of your native tongue you would babble and scream and do all sorts of things and you would communicate after a fashion only because the "gods" — that is in this analogy "adults" — can approximately tell what you're getting at. But, you're going to be largely ineffective in your communication because you have not yet recognized the constraints, meaningful constraints, of proper sounds much less words and sentences.

So effective meta-communication takes place in a way similar to ordinary verbal communication occurs and that is under the constraints of some kind of rules, and that's where true genius and true creativity can take place.

As I have said many times, you can't recognize a good athlete if there are no rules to the game. If you say: "Look at that guy block on the offensive line," and if people know how such things are done and the science of that activity as performed within the rules of the game of football, then they can look at a player and say, "That is a true athlete, he is a truly accomplished player." Now if you said there are no rules to how you're supposed to accomplish this feat, then the guy would just bring an iron bar or something and break the knee of the guy who's trying to come across the line. He's not coming across this line, he's not gonna sack my quarterback! Our lineman would just use his iron bar or a gun to stop his opponent. That would be easy, but there would be no skill, no grace in it, there would be nothing but brute force. In a world without the constraint of rules everything would be ruled by such force. But the realm of spirit is beyond physical power. Intelligence guides and directs and creates physical power but it itself is beyond it, therefore it is full of the kind of thing that in this world we only see in art and in the intellect and in philosophical arguments and things of that nature.

In a practical sense, in order to practice traditional rune magic in modern English one would naturally use, English Runes, Old English Runes, if you will. These characters are just as good for writing modern English as they were for writing our ancient tongue. In fact they are better than the Roman alphabet we now use. But we would reserve the runic system of writing for esoteric purposes, as it was so restricted in the past. The use of Old English Runes for magical communication has been insufficiently explored and made manifest. One might protest: "That's not traditional — using *modern* English for rune-magic ... I've never heard of that!"

But of course you have because that is precisely what all of the old inscriptions: are rune-masters writing runes in their own language. Archaized sometimes for poetic purposes, but that is exactly what they were doing. They were not writing in a language other than their own when they wrote a runic inscription, they wrote in their own language, in their own runes. So I say traditional rune magic involves, at least in part, writing runes in your own language in your own runes. Fortunately we have, as English speakers, our own runes, those are the aptly named English Runes, Old English Runes or Anglo-Saxon Runes. So in traditional rune magic, in writing actual texts, one would tend *not* to use the Older Futhark or the Younger Futhark when writing in English. That is incorrect, that is disharmonious, that is out of keeping with tradition. The older runic system is used for Proto-Germanic or Primitive Norse messages or runes in isolation. The Younger Futhark is used for writing in Icelandic or in Old Scandinavian dialects. The older language or modern Icelandic could easily be written in Younger Futhark Runes. So if one wants to learn Icelandic, which I would encourage anyone who has the opportunity to do, then the use of the Younger Futhark becomes a natural, harmonious, and beautiful exercise not a disjointed kind of inauthentic exercise of combining modern English with older runes, for example. Such a thing is very ugly I would say, it is not aesthetically pleasing in a spiritual way. But writing in English Runes, the use of the English language is natural and harmonious. Your options are fully open and you can discover and gain esoteric insight into all of the runes in that rich tradition. This is part of the subject matter of my recent book *Alu*.

There is also another element of traditional rune magic, which is that of accessing deeper traditions. We need to make deeper discoveries based on the *primary sources of runic knowledge*. What has tended to happen up to now is people just keep writing the same beginning rune book over and over. Different authors jump on the bandwagon, but nothing of value is added. There is a book I wrote that is a prime example of the exploration of primary sources. This book is entitled *The Rune Poems*. This volume is the mother-load of all knowledge of primary sources of all kinds of runic material. This book includes not only the major rune poems but the obscure runic poems, a Latin gloss system that was discovered, a little-known Swedish Rune poem, and then also the *Málrúnakenningar*. This latter body of lore consists of systems of *magical alphabets* in Icelandic magic books, which are keyed to the alphabetic system but which also have lore attached to each character. This lore is clearly derived from runic sources. So using all of that material in a systematic way to gain as deep an insight into the primary sources is a key to the traditional approach.

There are other places to look for treasures as well.

For example, if we look at *uruz* and then we read in Caesar's *De bello Gallico* in the section where he talks about the Germanic peoples, and discusses young men hunting the aurochs, which is *uruz*, as a rite of passage. He tells us they go and have to hunt this animal and kill it in their primitive way. I mean obviously it was quite a challenge and a lot of young men died I'm sure in that process. They hunted these animals for their meat, of course, but also for their horns which they used in ceremonies and things of that nature. Here we get a good bit of *uruz*-lore, about that secret or mystery as encoded in the behavior of the culture which had it as a name for one of their mysteries— the *uruz*, the aurochs. And there we discover in a Latin manuscript of the first century B.C.E. a source of insight relevant to runelore. This kind of lore is everywhere. We find it in all kinds of texts, Latin and Greek works about the Germanic peoples, the Eddas and sagas, in the later folklore and in archeology. So from a variety of sources we can glean *primary*, basic, data about rune-lore. This is not the speculation of others, but the primary data. And upon that primary data we gain insight and it becomes an organic part of us and it expands our knowledge-base as far as the runes are concerned.

This is the process which supports the books I write. Although I would not footnote everything in a book of operative or contemplative runology — they are not very attractive to most people — and footnotes are really not appropriate for that kind of book. But if someone set me down and asked: "Why did you write that sentence about this rune?" I can guarantee you in every instance I could tell you what the primary source for that was and what the insight was and how that eventuated itself as a sentence, or as an idea as expressed on the page.

In a manner of speaking this is rather akin to a math problem wherein you show the work done to arrive at a given answer. The answer is one thing, but the connective tissue between the conclusion or the insight and the primary source is essential when dealing with culture. This connectivity within the tradition forms the basis and the nexus of what I would term Traditional Rune Magic.

V
The Utility of Objective Traditions

The idea of the objectivity of tradition was also addressed to some extent by me in the now rare volume entitled *Red Rûna*.

Objective tradition: let us focus on that for a second. I think from earlier talks, you probably have a very good idea of what it is I am talking about, but let us contrast it here first with subjective traditions. Can there be such things as "subjective traditions"?

Yes, of course there can be such things.

That is, for example, when someone who shall remain nameless at this point, comes up and takes the Runic system and says: "Ok, I'm gonna just throw them out here, these runes here, on the ground or table," or whatever it was, "and come up with a new order for them, then write a book about this new order of things, and say this is what I'm teaching." Well, that approach was subjective. That was this *one individual's* singular experience. It was a private result, arbitrary to that person at that time and place when he cast the runes. But then this one reading was taught to others as a universal truth. In other words, something personal and arbitrary can imitate a "tradition" because other people reading it learn it and thus pass it on. But it was based on a *subjective* model, not an objective one. Similarly when someone bases a *religion* or a philosophy on the works of the science fiction writer H.P. Lovecraft; even though he might not have intended for people to do such things, obviously. His mythos nevertheless becomes a subjective tradition, although it was merely the creation of his singular mind. What do we learn when we unravel such a tradition?

We learn about the hidden dimensions, and the deep, inner recesses, of the creator's mind. The creator's mind, that is the non-traditional rune-writer's mind or Lovecraft's mind. J.R.R. Tolkien's alternate universe was created based in part, to be sure, on old Germanic models. He was, after all, a professor of Old English and Old Norse studies and as such he was informed by that material. But it was not his intention to represent this tradition directly. Rather it was something of his own artistic creation, so that when we unravel that "mythic universe" what we are really delving into and discovering, more than anything else, is the artistic imagination of Tolkien, or the mind of Lovecraft or the mind of the random rune writer. We aim to be informed by the tradition, not by the mind of an individual, ancient or modern.

The objective tradition is based on a historically valid, independently verifiable, transpersonal tradition. This is something which has already stood the test of time over centuries. In its own day it was recognized as being some kind of divine revelation from the gods. This connection can be reforged today. Knowledge can be derived from this source on a regular day-in-day-out basis today. Such access to special knowledge was reserved to a special elite in ancient times. Today, however, tradition is being taken up and used of by people who are not using these traditions for more than what appears to be recreational purposes. As practiced by most people today; magic, or religion, or all kinds of things of that nature, are not a matter of life-or-death survival. Rather they are luxuries which people indulge in, often as forms of amusement or entertainment. In ancient times these traditions were not luxuries, they were the backbone of our survival and success, and so they were usually very useful and practical things. Here we have to stop and think about the nature of objective *versus* subjective traditions.

Why do we want to use an objective tradition as opposed to a subjective one?

Can we get similar results using one rather than the other?

I would say no. As long as things remain recreational, and that is as far as anything goes, perhaps. Maybe there is little distinction between the two. But if it becomes a matter of life and death for you individually— spiritual or physical life and death, or life and death for a whole culture or for a group, things are different. Let's say things in this world do go to pot and we live in a "Mad Max" world. What is going to hold people together as an effective culture when all our luxuries break down?

The answer is that it will be the same thing people utilized in ancient times when no such luxuries existed. This is the only plausible, reliable answer. Those people who are able to organize themselves and motivate themselves and others to be, and remain, organized and to aim for higher purposes and focus on values transcendental to their present circumstance will be those who will not only survive, but who will thrive and will become successful. Technology is not the answer. If we look back into ancient times we see some examples of that. It is not necessarily the technologically superior society which gains victory over another, nor is it the more culturally advanced one, it is the one which has the stronger sense of identity and solidarity and the one willing and able to put these qualities into action. They will have an almost irrational solidarity within and among themselves, and a belief, even an irrational belief, in themselves and their special destiny. Of course, all this is actually very rational because it is what provides the margin of victory, the margin of success if you will, the *sigrsæll*, so that the culture is successful. Using objective criteria in the choice of tradition is something that is inherently the superior choice. It is akin to saying I'm going to be flying an airplane in the dark at night, with no instruments. What if I have no instruments and I'm in the dark and I'm using a subjective tradition?

On such a flight the cockpit conversation might go something like this:

"It feels like the ground is here or there ... it kinda ... what do you think Joe? What does your crystal ball say there?"

Boom!

All of a sudden they are in the water or on the side of a mountain.

So what are the objective signs, what are the guideposts along the path to show your way in the dark?

What are the instruments?

They are the criteria of the tradition. They provide you with your instruments, the abstract principles by which you can even fly in the dark. In the daytime correct observation of physical points of reference guide you on your way. So the lower, physical observations of nature as well as instrumentalities of higher caliber guide you. These latter tools are analogous to the objective tradition, whereas the former tend to be observations of nature or of objective historical facts. This process protects you for being put in a dangerous situation, and so the absurdity becomes obvious whenever anyone says: "Now I'm going to worship Cthulhu."

In the end even the very purpose of the recreational religion of Cthulhu worship ends with you being gobbled up by the monster. Which is fun, if you are not going to be serious about it. It is rather like riding in an amusement park ride or going to see a Freddy Kruger movie. But that is not what culture is based on. Ideally we would like to have something which would provide the things needed for a healthy culture for anyone at all times. This is especially true when you think of an individual or a culture in crisis. What are you going to rely upon? So we ask ourselves what is the utility, or the practical reason, for using one of these objective traditions, such as the Runic tradition; with its Fuþark divided in a certain way, and with runes named in a definite manner, and with all of the attendant lore — all in the matrix of the mythology of Óðinn and all the other gods and goddesses of Ásgarðr, with the cosmology of Yggdrasill, and all of the things that are historically valid, independently verifiable bodies of complex structure and all the complex elements which we can work on for a lifetime? What is the *utility of*, and not just merely esthetic choice of, engaging with one of these types of traditions rather that a subjective one which is our own creation or the adoption of some other subjective one where we believe in the wholesale invention of some individual?

The objective criteria that the traditional approach provides constitute a testing ground for the intellectual and cultural insights one might have. You can test your insight against some kind of matrix of meaning where you can get feedback saying, "Yes I'm on the right track. If I think this, if I gain this insight and make this connection then I look at this other data over here, part of the same organism, and it makes more sense today with this insight than it did yesterday without it. So I am gaining meaningful connective material to show that this is working."

This is akin to a laboratory or your own personal developmental, inner laboratory.

Here and now in this world we are living in now is where most of us are with our activities. In the ancient world the testing ground was indeed the world itself. The ancient Romans, for example, thrived and were an extremely successful culture not because of their technological superiority — although they did have some technological innovations — but really that was not their base. Their cultural base was in their discipline. For example, in the field of battle in their use of certain tactics which involved recruiting men, maintaining them, maintaining their motivation, training them, and so forth. It was not a matter of technology. The Celts, for example, had superior iron to the Romans in the beginning, but their society was disorganized and each clan fought for itself and old grudges against one another would sometimes play themselves out on the battlefield. So when the Romans started getting the better of one clan, the other clans might say, "We are not going to help that clan, I never liked them anyway," and would just get up and leave. There was little if any inter-clanic solidarity among them.

What do we mean by solidarity?

Solidarity is provided by myth. That is a part of the mythology of Rome, it provides an identity for them, a sense of solidarity, and beyond that in the case of the Roman army, of discipline and of martial training as a unit. They fought as a unit. These things are not technology *per se*, these are cultural phenomena, these are cultural features which are learned, ingrained, and passed on. This is what provided the Romans with their military superiority. Similarly in the Fall of Rome, of course, that system, like all systems tend to do, had become decadent and defunct. The Romans, of course, had superior military technology and techniques and things that they had learned over time but they lost their cultural cohesion and their mythology. For example, they had become Christian and that shocked their cultural sense of uniqueness, of superiority, of solidarity. They started to question: "What does it mean to be a Roman? Anybody and their uncle is a Roman today," and so they lost their nerve, they lost their cultural nerve. And, of course, we live in a time where our culture and our generation in this past half century has lost its nerve and so we live in a world where this nerve is increasingly being lost before our eyes. So through the observation of analogous historical situations we can gain insight and knowledge into a world like that of Rome at the time of the Fall of the Roman Empire.

We look back and observe the prelude to the present demise, or the last phase in which we did have our nerve, in the time of the Second World War. Here we are not speaking about the justifications for the War on the part of the Allies, we are just looking at an example of a culture which possessed its nerve. It was a culture with a sense of purpose, solidarity within itself, an identity as "American" and solidarity with all things "American." This period of the Second World War and its immediate aftermath was the last hurrah of all that.

Although almost everyone reading this was not alive during this time, those who were can clearly remember it. You could see it and feel this quality in the culture and in the lives of our parents and grandparents. The contrast between that cultural feeling and the present one is profound. We can feel the difference between a culture which has not lost its nerve and one which has. And what is better?

It is better to *have* your nerve.

It is better to have that sense of identity and solidarity with your neighbors rather than not have it. What? I hear someone out there saying: "NO! It's better to have *no* nerve, to have *lost* your nerve that makes for a better, a fairer and more equitable society."

Stop and think about what you just thought and see how crazy it is, and you probably really do not want to be crazy.

Other examples of cultures with robust nerve include the so-called Vikings. They had some technological innovations which gave them an edge such as their ships, and so on. But really it was the way they were organized— and they were very organized. Look at the invasion of England they mounted. The camps in Denmark from which they set off to England were models of organization. They were highly structured. They would make a Roman envious of the level of organization and discipline they had. They set out on an adventurous mission with great purpose supported by a magnificent and heroic mythology. They certainly were a culture which not only had *not* lost its nerve— they were nerve incarnate. So we see them today and wonder: if we could regain just a modicum of what they left to us in the form of artifacts of word and object then we will surely be the better for it.

Thinking of them, if we project ourselves into our future and flippantly say it will be like a *Mad Max*-world where all of our niceties are broken down. We begin to wonder: Who will succeed?

Who will have victory?

Who will emerge?

It is those who have their nerve, who have their traditions, who have purpose, direction, sense of solidarity among themselves, a sense of identity with something greater than themselves— those are the ones that will succeed. Such people may be good, or they may be not so good. But they will thrive. Therefore what we fight for today, and what we encourage today, are the traditions which will provide the *edge* and which will — we hope — be in the hands of those who are on the side of the good. But there is always an intrinsic good in just being on your *own* side and not being a self-destructive people. In the world of the ancients, or in the world of a possible future, a self-destructive people is not long for this world.

VI
Two Forms of Immortality

Immortality is one of man's greatest quests. People have searched for things such as the Holy Grail, the Fountain of Youth, and so on, and it is always for immortality that this quest is set out. Man's mortality constitutes one of the great *secrets* of humanity— our self-awareness of death. Not that we die so much *per se*, but that we are *aware* of our eventual demise. All things that are born, live and pass away. This is true whether it is a bacterium or a human being. All those things, all things that live also die. As far as we know, again, only the human being is aware of impending death, inevitable death, and so individuals have from the dawn of this awareness struggled for immortality.

Throughout history there was the idea that immortality could be gained but this was something that came only after a long search or after a long protracted amount of work. People often ask, "How did Christianity gain such a foothold among our people, it being such a vacuous and empty sort of philosophy of life? How did it gain such a foothold?"

Given that man's mortality weighs upon him, given that a quest for immortality is one of his greatest dreams, and given the fact that the majority of humanity is extremely lazy, an answer begins to emerge. Once somebody realized that you could sell someone a package of goods that said, "If you do these very simple and easy things you'll be immortal. You will have life everlasting. And did I mention that it's simple, it's easy. It's really just a trick of your mind, just *believe*, there's no work involved it's just a quick and easy type of fix to this enormous weighty problem." The trap was set.

A lot of people went for it, obviously. It has a compelling appeal, but that does not necessarily make it true. We would prefer to stick with the prevailing wisdom of the ages and simply say that immortality is possible, but it is something that the individual must work for. It is not something which is necessarily granted by a higher power; although I will not deny this possibility at all. As the Utterer of the word *Rûna*, I will be the last one to say this or that is categorically impossible and that something such as a god granting immortality is impossible. I would not say that. I would simply say that to believe that one must work for such things is a more solid basis to proceed from in life and one that results in a better world rather than believing in magic fairy-dust that will solve all of your problems suddenly and without work or effort.

Man's quest for immortality is somewhat reflected pessimistically in the Rune Poems where it says, "*Maðr er moldar auki,*" that is, "man is the augmentation of the earth." When he is buried he becomes part of the Earth. So this idea that to be human is to also to be mortal is fundamental to the understanding of humanity. So we recognize death in a realistic way, we see it, we do not wish to deny it, but rather recognize it in a realistic way. We want to look at the possibilities it opens us up to, and also for the end that it brings to the present life.

In my book on *Johannes Bureus and Adalruna,* I note that he quotes from a Hermetic source concerning two kinds of souls in a way that I think is relevant to the idea of immortality:

"Those chosen by God are of two kinds. The one
are those who migrate the other those who are
still and these are the highest, holiest of souls."

This seems to refer to maintaining an awareness, an eternal awareness, and says that these are two kinds of immortality: a migratory form and a static form of immortality.

A static form of immortality is essentially that which Christianity seems to promise and they are not the first to have done so. All sorts of religions promising immortality to the masses understand immortality in this frame of reference. The belief is that I myself, as a being who is aware of my own individuality and personhood, will not die, that this self-awareness and ego-consciousness will somehow go on beyond the death of my physical body and I will be aware of myself as this particular individual and I personally will gain immortality. In the religion from which Judaism, and then Christianity, took many of its doctrines — Zoroastrianism — the idea was developed that there would actually be a resurrection of your individual physical body in a future state which will be immortal. Now that is an astounding idea and one that is certainly a matter of deep faith. Faith would be needed to believe such an amazing idea. The reason the Zoroastrians insisted upon this doctrine was that they thought that *matter* — contrary to many people's misconceptions about Zoroastrianism — was intrinsically *good* and had been created by the Good God and that there would be a return — an eternal return — of forms to their original state only now perfected through the cycles of history into a perfected form— into an immortal form. This is what characterizes the divine world or divine state. Things are at their ultimate level of permanence, their ultimate level of beauty, their ultimate of perfection. Therefore the idea of the resurrection of the body is a *logical* conclusion within the frame-work of Zoroastrianism. Given that there would be an evolution of the cosmos into an ever more perfect state under the guidance of the Good God or the Wise Lord— Ahura-Mazda.

But Jews later absorbed this idea within their mythology and then Christians did also. But as a religious idea it did not quite make the transition because in these later monotheistic religions the idea that all humans are people who have *chosen* the Good and whose spiritual selves have come here to fight the good fight is obviously missing. This willingness to fight for the Good is why human beings are here on the Earth at all. The fact that you are here is a certification of your essential goodness and your ultimate immortality. That is much too optimistic for systems bent on manipulating people to do the will of the "powers that be"— and this is the code of Judaism and Christianity (as well as Islam, obviously). This Mazdan optimism was unacceptable. So the idea that some will be condemned to Hell — in fact, almost all — but *you*, if *you* buy our product and you're a true believer and you're one of the chosen ones, special and different from all the others, *you* will gain immortality. But you have to buy now, don't wait, supplies are running out. That kind of "hard-sell" manipulation was employed throughout history, and thus blasphemed and corrupted this otherwise beautiful idea. Notice that the Mazdan myth makes it so that Man chose the Good, whereas the Judeo-Christian myth has God being the one who choses. The Abrahamic religions are based on the idea that Man (Adam) made the *wrong* choice, and was condemned as an eternal sinner who deserves death.

In the static form of immortality, regardless of whatever else we can say about it, the fact remains that what we are talking about is that the mind of the subject — the mind of the person — remains intact forever. This is obvious in this ideology, but you also see it in vampire mythology, and in mummy mythology in pop-culture. An idea I talked about in one of the old broadcasts of Radio Free Rûna concerned an illustration of these two forms of immortality found in the "mummy movies" produced by Universal in the 1940s. There you have the idea of the mummy eternally himself, Kharis (= the Gift), and then the Princess Ananka, a Greek word meaning "Need"— the same thing as the Germanic *naudiz*, meaning "need" or "distress." This idea of the static form of immortality is one in which the persona is immortal, so that you are aware of your personhood forever. But stop and think about this for a minute: this idea really fulfills the Christian ideal of destroying culture. It is a secret methodology for the destruction of traditional, intricate, authentic culture because—and it is something that people will "buy" immediately because this is what they quest for—they quest for *personal* immortality. Why do they do this? It is because they *fear* death. A system comes along and offers to alleviate them of this fear, to each one individually, "Take it now, that's what you're looking for and I'm offering it!" Of course it is only being offered in a fraudulent way, but once the truth is known, no one is in a position to demand a refund. The average person will tend to believe in this deal, if offered. We see in the story of the Frisian king Radbod, that he, as an ideal Germanic king, did not take the deal. When he was going to be baptized and they said, "You will now be immortal and on the right hand side of God," he then asked the good question, "Where will my ancestors be? Where will all of the other kings of Frisia be when I am sitting on the right hand side of God?"

And the priest answers, "They'll be in Hell with all the other pagans and ne'er-do-wells of the universe."

And he then kicks the priest in the rear end and gets him out of the kingdom and says, "I had rather be in Hell with the kings of Frisia than in Heaven with a bunch of beggars." Here we have someone who is expressing the idea of cultural identity, solidarity, and who is willing and able to act in this spirit. He is maintaining an integral, authentic culture, and being the standard-bearer for that idea in his actions.

How does this individualistic immortality, and the promise of it in the Christian guise, with its hard-sell pitch of, "most will go to Hell but you're going to Heaven, if you buy now, don't wait, supplies are running out," lead to negative consequences in the culture? If you "buy" this belief, the culture will be eroded and be slowly destroyed because if the individual can opt out of belonging to the organic family and be "saved," or made immortal and separate from the tribe, then the average subject has no more interest in the health or well-being of the tribe or the Earth or anything else. This is because they are going to be taken away by the Space Brothers. They are just waiting for the spaceship to take them away, and so they don't really care about you or anything else. In our history this way of thinking begins with the coming of Christianity. It does not begin with Zoroastrianism and the prophet Zarathustra— although the promise of immortality of the individual is an invention, like almost all of religion, of the Zoroastrians. The idea was misused in that Zarathustra says that all humans are ultimately destined for perfection and salvation. The fact that we are here as conscious and self-aware human beings is a confirmation of that fact in his ideology. With Christianity this is not the case, rather it is said that only a few will make it and most will not, most are going to Hell and you need to get on the right side of this, you need to obey authority, behave the way it tells you to— otherwise you're out. President Reagan had a Secretary of the Interior, I think his name was James Watt, and Congress was questioning him one time before one of their show-hearings about some environmental issues and he said these things really didn't matter to him too much, because the Lord is coming back soon and all of this environmental stuff is just not that important. So people really believe this kind of dogma, and when they do it cannot be good, in the sense that it is irresponsible. Even if it *is* true — which of course it probably is not — but nevertheless, let's just put on our little fantasy caps and say it is true. Nevertheless, would it not be better to be responsible rather than irresponsible?

Would it not be better to avoid the use of this doctrine as a way to behave in an irresponsible way towards our fellow man or towards our environment, etc.?

Well, of course, yes! The answer is yes. But man's inherent laziness and disregard for things allows man to use these kinds of doctrines immediately, enthusiastically, and universally as excuses to shirk their responsibilities. I have a phrase I use often in conversation as an analysis of our world today, and I see confirmation of it on a daily basis the term is "Shirker-Nation." That's what we are, a Shirker-Nation. Everyone is looking and seeking, not for immortality, not for perfection, but a way to shirk their responsibilities so they can veg out and acquire slack. The highest good is to get your neighbor to assume your responsibilities. So that is the way of the modernistic world my friends, and we are bound to attempt to change it. In essence this turn of events stems from the Christian dogma of individual salvation and the forgiveness of sins by means of simple mind-tricks.

Another form of immortality is the dynamic form, this is not the static form wherein the personality of the individual lasts forever but rather a dynamic form of immortality. And this is most often identified with reincarnation. That is, something of the self trans-migrates from one material body to another. Of course there are many pop-culture ideas about this which became popular in the 20th century which have no traditional basis but which many people who believe in reincarnation do indeed believe. One of the chief beliefs is that your soul, through no effort of your own, will simply go from this body to one in China, and back to an Eskimo, and down to a South American, or whatever and it will just pop around the globe according to some random nature. This is a "new idea," by which I mean an illegitimate idea, and so it has no traditional basis at all. There are of course cultures and religions which have reincarnation as a is fundamental part of their doctrines. For example, Hinduism or Buddhism, and these both have their origins in something deeper and broader which is the Indo-European idea of reincarnation. Nevertheless you will find in contemporary Hindu or Buddhistic culture that people believe in reincarnation as a fundamental doctrine of their religion. However, you will not often find people saying to Hindus, "Well, what you need to do is a past-live regression there Samu."

Why would he do that?

He is born to a particular caste or position in life — in a hierarchy of souls — and he knows who and where he is so he therefore also knows in essence where he came from and knows in essence where he is bound to spend his efforts aiming for. Everything which is essential is known to him by his birth. He does not need to think, "Well I was burned as a witch back in the 1600s so that's why I'm afraid of fire today..." Things like that made up some of the common 1970s verbiage, I'm afraid. But when you look at traditions and religions which actually hold traditional doctrines of "reincarnation" and compare and contrast them with the New Age idea about these things you quickly see there is a great and glaring gulf between the two.

The original idea of reincarnation — or dynamic immortality — as I might phrase it, is in the Indo-European ideology. We see it exemplified in the Germanic world. Many people reading this are already familiar with this idea that one is reborn within a genetic chain, within a clan, or family, etc. The fact that this was the ancient belief is not debatable. It is fundamentally ingrained in the saga literature of the Icelanders, for example. It is also demonstrated in the naming practices of the ancient Germanic peoples wherein new offspring, newborn children, are systematically named after dead ancestors. This was done in the belief that this child is in fact that ancestor, in essence, reborn.

The idea of, and the fact of, the phenomenon of death is fundamental to the dynamic form of immortality. There must be death in order to have rebirth, there must be death in order to be reborn. There must be a disincarnation in order for there to be a reincarnation. Therefore, this dynamic form of immortality constitutes a shedding of non-essential components of life. Just like a snake sheds its skin in order to grow. This process allows for actual, factual renewal. You are actually made *new* again. Why? Who would want to grow eternally old? In the ancient Germanic way of thinking, in ancient Indo-European way of thinking, this is not desirable. Once we get old we are old. Your mind is old. I don't want to live on as an 80 year old, a 100 year old, a 500 year old forever. It sounds like a form of Hel to me, rather I would want to be actually renewed. In fact want to forget much of what I have learned. I don't want to lose what I have gained *in essence*, but forget much of what I have seen, forget much of what I have been programmed to receive, etc.

Yes, because then you have the possibility of actually experiencing freshness, a new day, a new life in reality. Just being immortal in the same mind would not be pleasurable, I believe. This whole question is something I ask anyone reading this to contemplate. Do not let doctrines or past personal beliefs interfere in your thoughts, contemplate without fear. Ultimately the fear of death is the fear of the Unknown. Those who Seek Rûna make friends with the Unknown, and tend not to fear death so much. Those who fear death also often have an underlying fear of transformation of any kind. There are still days when I can conjure a fear of death. I can feel the fear of that idea because I am still not that old, and have much yet to do. But I notice that when people do get older and older they seem to lose their fear of death naturally, it seems to be a biological program. But when we think about eternal life without death, without change, it becomes unattractive really. And so there are other times when I think, "Well why not step through that door and see what's on the other side," and it becomes almost a magnetic attraction. There is repulsion and attraction at the same time.

It is hoped that a younger person would feel complete repulsion at the idea of death because they already feel themselves to be immortal. They are going to live forever; and that is what is healthy and good for a 20 year old. For a 50-, or 60-year old such as I am at this point, perhaps we are in a middle phase between attraction and repulsion. Whereas in the end of life, we see death as a precursor to our renewal so we may be strangely attracted by it.

In the words of Bela Lugosi in *Dracula* (1931), "To die, to be truly dead, that would be wonderful." From the psychology of someone who is in the static form of immortality perhaps this is true. With dynamic immortality the possibility exists for the experience of truly *new* life, unencumbered by the *memories* of the past. When we look back into traditional cultures such as the Old Icelandic or Germanic we see that the function of myth and traditional family histories called the Sagas in ancient times, were really there to provide individuals with all that they *needed* with regard to memory about their own pasts. These were needed in order to know what was necessary, to know what was real, so that they might know what needed to be done. Everything they needed to know was provided by myth and personal and traditional family histories.

VII
Two Forms of Reincarnation

In the last essay we wrote about immortality and touched upon the idea of reincarnation. Now here I would like to write about two forms of this process, a process which in the ancient Germanic world was called *aptrburðr*.

Historical and culturally authentic forms of belief in reincarnation are present for us to study. In history we see that the Germanic ideal of reincarnation, or *aptrburðr*, was something which took place within a clan and in a family, or tribe, in other words it has a genetic component. It is quite obvious and natural that someone would look at his child and see the traits of his dead grandfather or great grandfather or of whomever, and in seeing these genetic similarities assume that *something* of the ancestor was being *reborn* in the descendent. And of course something *is*. DNA is handed on, or what the ancients poetically called "the blood." One could see there was a genetic connection even though they knew nothing of genetics in the scientific sense. They knew everything which is *necessary* to know about it simply through animal breeding, family histories, and so forth. So they came to believe in this idea, and this belief was reinforced in their mythology and ideology. We see the manifestation of this belief in ancient naming practices. Newborn children were named after dead ancestors. This kept up an idea of not only cultural continuity but family continuity also, as long as people believed this. It was not something debatable or a matter of subjective speculation. People did not ask "Oh, what do you think there Einarr? Do you think we can survive death, do you think we are immortal?"

The truth was self-evident to them.

When people say: "Well, Christianity offered immortality to these pagans and that's why they bought it." They are misinformed.

Pagans "bought" because it was *easy*, not because it offered something that had never been offered before. But because it offered it at such a cheap price, they had a hard time passing it up. This ease of achievement played on their fears of personal mortality or *persona* mortality, and for some people, until they reach a certain age, or stage of development, death can cause great fear.

So there were various psychological reasons why this scenario was attractive. But to say that Christianity offered immortality where the pagan systems did not is a categorical lie. Obviously the mystery religions as well as folk beliefs contained the idea of immortality. Furthermore it was not something which was a matter of wild-ass speculation, or belief, or faith. A man might look at his son as he grew up and say, "He has a lot of traits of his granddaddy and I can see it in his mannerisms, in the way he looks, and so on, and everyone can see it so in my mind it is not a matter of debate as to whether there is immortality. It stands before me in the form of my son who is the spit'n image of his grand-daddy."

All this had convinced them in a way beyond anything which modern man contemplates, of the continuity of culture in genetic form, in flesh and blood within the family or tribe or clan. This was unquestioned until the demise of that belief system under the force of the enormous and irresistible force of *human laziness.*

Then there are historical examples of the doctrine of reincarnation in religions which are not necessarily ancient, organic traditions, but rather ones developed by prophets. There is a little known sect, under Persian influence in Lebanon especially, called the Druzes and they believe in reincarnation. When I was teaching Humanities at Austin Community College I had quite a number of Druze students. One took my course and liked it so much he told all of his Druze friends After that all his Druze buddies and buddetts started to take my course. I got to know a number of them and they would tell me stories about their families and things back in Lebanon. One told me a story which was rather interesting: In their neighborhood which was in the battle-zone between all the warring factions in southern Lebanon, especially in the Beqaa Valley, there was a child who was killed by a bomb or a missile or something. He was a young child. Then a few days latter in a neighboring house down the street a child was born. Several years past and the people in the neighborhood noticed that — according to the story — this child had a lot of the characteristics of the child that was killed by the bomb. It became so obvious that this child was in fact the dead child reincarnated that the family of the boy actually gave up the child to the family of the boy who had been killed and said: "This is obviously really your child that we bore, and so he needs to come back home to you."

This demonstrates the depth of this idea in the form of a religious cult. This is not necessarily a folk tradition although, of course, it has become such a tradition for those people. This is quite interesting because those are not people who read Shirley MacLaine books or who get their ideas off late night A.M. talk radio. Rather these are deeply ingrained ideas which move people to act not simply to dream and shiver.

Modernistic ideas concerning this whole topic of reincarnation are of course all a bastardization of the idea, so you end up with people saying, "Oh, I had a past life regression the other day and it turned out I was actually Napoleon. Isn't that just marvelous?"

Yea, everybody's Napoleon or Cleopatra or something in these deals. I always wondered why all of these greats of history were so boring now. I guess the modern world just bums them out. Such regression fantasies can be useful therapeutically in the sense that you can get people to imagine freely and so from their fantasies you can learn something about their personalities, we suppose. But as far as traditions or facts or anything real or authentic we can just write it off.

There are actually two traditional forms of reincarnation. Both are supported by ancient doctrines. One is organic. It is simply genetic. You are your ancestors or an ancestor reborn. This soul has flowed down to you in a river of DNA that forms the matrix into which the non-natural, spiritual component is meshed because of their similarities in form and structure. This metaphysic is one of the reasons why the ancient Germanic peoples often practiced cremation. In the Ibn Fadlan report it says that an informant told him that "we burn the body so that he goes immediately to paradise." The soul goes immediately to a higher state or another state, immediately as opposed to allowing the body to rot slowly in the ground the way the Arabs and Christians and such people treat their dead. The Germanic peoples did this to free the soul from the matrix of the body. This also explains the common stories about the *aptrgöngumenn*, the men who walk again after death. They are dead but come back to life out of the grave. They wander about the countryside often causing mischief. The people in Haiti call them similar men *zombis* and so forth. These are walking dead corpses like a vampire or something. So we ask ourselves how is this possible in the metaphysic of the ancient peoples?

It is simple really. At death, part of the soul, the animating principle, is separated from the body— this is what constitutes death. But this soul will try to reincarnate, it will try to find a physical matrix which is a highly receptive vessel for it due to the similarities between it and a human body as an attractor. The body acts in a way similar to an antenna. And so the soul will tend to come back to its former body, or a body-configuration very similar to its old one. If we look at central European Jewish folklore, you have the idea of the *dybbuk* where a dead person comes back and — temporarily at least — incarnates in a family member. The living family member begins to take on the mannerisms of the dead person. Again we ask ourselves: Why a family member?

In folklore it is said that the vampire comes back first to its own family. This is a reflection of the belief, or the idea, which is a fairly solid one, that there is a similarity structurally between the spiritual component and the physical component and when these are separated by death there will remain a natural attraction or affinity between these similar systems. The soul is attracted to bodies encoded in a way similar to itself and to the previous physical existence. So one's old body, or that of a family member becomes attractive to the discarnate soul. The ancient Germanic peoples ritually harnessed this natural tendency with their beliefs, birth rituals and naming practices.

This model of linkage between systems of similar kinds of things is also a fundamental notion of any form of communication or any kind of broadcast and reception of signals of any kind, shape or form. The systems must be similar in order for the link to be made. Dissimilarity in systems makes communication difficult or impossible. Our ancestors had no conscious idea about some of the things I'm alluding to, but nevertheless they *understood* them and they — if we believe the stories in any way — apparently *experienced* them, observed their results and had ways of using them in practical ways.

Thus there are two forms of immortality, one is organic. It is simply the rebirth of ancestors in newly born descendants. The other is a free-form of reincarnation in which the soul of the incarnate being today will enter freely into a newborn child independent of the genetic link between this body and the previous body to which the soul in question was attached. This pattern too is actually supported by ancient Germanic ideology, where the *hamingja* of one person is passed to another person intentionally and willfully. So both forms in question were known in antiquity. It is just that the one with the genetic link is natural and ordinary, where as the other free-form one is extraordinary and heroic. The organic one supports the ordinary and natural flow of life, the free-form is something which is magical and initiatory. For example in the doctrines of Hinduism, where ideas of reincarnation are an ordinary part of the religion, we see the idea of *avatars*, of incarnations of beings because it is *necessary* for them to be incarnated in a certain time and place, because they have a special mission of some kind.

So when we look at the organic form of reincarnation we see that it is rooted in Indo-European ideology. It is very much supported by Germanic lore and history and we see it in the naming practices wherein newly born children are systematically named after dead ancestors. Even when you look at the etymology for the German word for a grandson, which is *Enkel*, it is seen to mean literally: "the little ancestor." *Ahne* is ancestor, *Enkel* is the little ancestor. We find it in the runic inscriptions, we see it in the name Attila, this is a Gothic name, or word, based on the diminutive form of the Gothic word for "father"— *atta*. The Gothic form of the Lord's Prayer begins: *Atta unsar*... This was the name of the famous Hunnic chieftain — many of the Huns had Gothic names because of the period of cultural intermixture between the Goths and Huns. The name literally means "little father." Who is the *big father* implied by this?

He is the higher one from whom this lower one comes. The little one is the one on Earth just like the little ancestor is the new one if he comes from a bigger one, an older one from earlier in the family tree. All this is explained, or this is supported and evidenced, by what we call genetics, obviously. And so whether it is reincarnation in the New

Age sense, or whether it is simply an explanation of how traits are inherited from previous generations, is rather a moot point because its purpose is to ensure the continuity of solidarity. Not only are people to have a sense of solidarity — in a good society, in the best of all possible societies — with their neighbors but also with their ancestors over time. Not just space, but also time should be the matrix of solidarity.

The free-form of reincarnation — that is where someone can reincarnate in a random, or seemingly random, child, who is perhaps genetically unconnected to the soul — is really a non-natural, willed act. It is something which is directed from a higher power, and here again we are reminded of the avatars in Hinduism. In Buddhism there are bodhisattvas who fulfill a similar function. We see it in our present day it is discussed openly and obviously in relation to the Dalai Lama, for example. He dies and then he is reincarnated somewhere, not in his son, if he should have one, but rather somewhere in another Tibetan which is the only possibility. His soul is transferred to a Tibetan somewhere nearby. So then there follows a quest to find who this child is. We hear folkloristic stories about that, but again, here we have an illustration of an authentic tradition in which these beliefs are fundamentally practiced and acted upon.

So when we get down to the practicalities of this reincarnation ideology, we see to maintain the organic form of reincarnation it is important for people to have offspring. This is because you want to have receptacles for the souls of the dead ancestors. That was one of the big reasons people had children, a spiritual reason anyway. So having children helps ensure the possibilities for this form of immortality. The free-form of reincarnation however is is enhanced by the source-soul having no offspring. In order to be maximally free in the *post mortem* state. This freedom comes about because it is more difficult to reincarnate freely, if one is attracted by one's own family line in an almost electro-magnetic way. So we see that in the original story of the *Völsunga Saga* — until it was corrupted for certain political reasons — it is shown that the greatest of all Germanic heroes, Sigurðr, died without offspring. Later it was said he had a daughter with Sigrdrífa whom he impregnated there on the mountain after he awakened her from her magical slumber. The saga writer of the form of the saga which survives to us wanted to give his lord, the Norwegian king, a genealogy which connected the king to the heroic blood-line of Sigurd. To do this an offspring had to be provided. If Sigurd actually died without offspring then that would be impossible so it was invented *ad hoc* so a blood-line could be continued from *the Sigurd-line*.

Originally this saga is a story about the generation and development of a divine heroic soul. Óðinn engenders the line, which is not all that remarkable at first. But the heroic qualities of the head of the Völsung clan gets progressively better and better, stronger and better through each incarnation of the heroic oversoul (*fylgja*) until finally this essence reaches its apex in the form of Sigurðr, the greatest, the ultimate, the last of his kind. And, of course, if he is the last of his kind he cannot have an offspring to start a process of degeneration all over again. So there we see the pattern for this idea of not having offspring so that one is free for either non-incarnation or incarnation in various places and times.

All this is quite esoteric I realize, however, it is something which is not unsupported by traditional sources. And that is what we always look back on— the *source* so that we can discover not only the source of ourselves but also our destinies.

VIII
Right Hand Path and Left Hand Path as *Cooperative* Systems

When we look at the terms Right Hand Path and Left Hand Path we see that in my work the distinction and the words and phrases in question occur only rarely and then mainly in the context of *Lords of the Left Hand Path*, which is of course a study of the practice of the Left Hand Path throughout history. Historically these terms, or ones akin to them, do occur in ancient times, especially in Eastern thought. By Eastern I mainly mean India and ideologies derived from India. In these schools of the East the Right Hand Path : Left-Hand Path distinction is overtly made and discussed in such terms. It is here that the origin of the philosophical use of these terms lies.

First we must define what we mean by Right Hand Path and Left Hand Path. Here we do not have to go into esoteric works so much to define them, if we just look at Mircea Eliade's book entitled *Yoga* we see them defined in terms of Right Hand Path and Left Hand Path distinctions in yogic practices. Left Hand Path being the *Vāmamārga* and the Right Hand Path being the *Dakshinachara* or *Dakshinamārga*. So what do those Sanskrit words mean and what do they imply?

Very simply put the Right Hand Path is the way of union. This is union of the soul of the individual with the higher or greater law or entity or god if you will, or nature, if you wanted to extend it to other theologies. It is the way of the union of the self with something other than the self. Conversely the Left Hand Path — the *Vāmamārga* — is the way of non-union, wherein the self remains independent of the laws and mechanisms of nature, of god, or whatever greater matrix of law or organization one might posit. So it is a way of independence of the human soul or self — the psyche — from the matrix of these other laws or organizations.

In the normal consensus of most peoples' way of thinking, and certainly in the 19th century and following, there arose an increasing animosity between the Right Hand Path and Left Hand Path as ways of going about spiritual practices. One was intrinsically evil, that being the Left Hand Path, and one intrinsically good, being the Right Hand Path. Those distinctions remain implicit especially in Western monotheistic culture. In the East it was more a matter of suspicion perhaps of the Left Hand Path to a certain extent, but certainly they — practitioners of the Left Hand Path — were not totally demonized or ostracized. It was seen as merely another tool in the "toolbox" of various spiritual endeavors. So it was an alternate way, one which might be disagreed with or not followed but not something characterized as intrinsically evil or something that needed to be eradicated. So at the inception of these terms there was a kind of symbiosis between the two and not the extreme antipathy between them characteristic of the mindset which also gave rise to things such as the Theosophical Society in the late 19th century.

We all recognize, or people might recognize who are spiritual practitioners of any sort, that there is some sort of utility of Right Hand Path techniques and philosophy to the practitioner of the Left Hand Path. That is, the Right Hand Path is an easier Path to follow, an easier Path in which to get results because you are enmeshed in the substance within which you are trying to get results— within your own body, within your own physical environment, etc. So it is easier. For example, in the philosophy of the Temple of Set, Right Hand Path techniques or technologies are referred to as White Magic as opposed to Black Magic which is the technique of the Left Hand Path. The Left Hand Path is precisely defined as *the subjective approach to the subjective universe* by Dr. Michael Aquino. Because Right Hand Path techniques or White Magic is often useful to the practitioner of Left Hand Path this means that there is intrinsically no moral prohibition to using Right Hand Path techniques for the practitioner of the Left Hand Path. However, the reverse might not always be the case.

Historically the Left Hand Path is necessary, or some element of Left Hand Path philosophy and practice in the world and in society is necessary, to the continuing existence of the Right Hand Path consensus. This is because without the Left Hand Path and its practitioners no evolution or any substantive change in anything would ever take place because no one would ever for a moment be able to step outside the mechanism in which they find themselves enmeshed. They could never "think outside" of the proverbial "box." Therefore they would never question any of the laws of their universe in which they exist, they would never question or deny or turn against or cause a revolution against any of the prevailing laws or regulations, either morally, or physically, or anything else. It would eternally be the case of thinking: "If man was meant to fly he'd be given wings," or whatever kind of platitudes that are typical of the pop culture of a Right Hand Path mentality. Human culture would be very much like an anthill. Ideally, in the absolute Right Hand Path universe all would know their places, everyone would do his role, there would be no questions asked. Whereas in an absolute Left Hand Path universe, if everything went in the other direction, there would be utter chaos and absolute disorder. There would be no sense of cooperation, no basis for cooperation between and among people because they would be practicing and implementing Left Hand Path philosophy far in excess of their philosophical or Initiatory ability to deal with the ideas and so chaos would ensue.

Therefore in reality a cooperation occurs so that each extreme rather tempers the opposing impulse. This is true and present in the life of an individual and the spiritual path of the individuals and it is also present, of course, in societies and collective bodies of individuals.

The Right Hand Path mentality is to a great extent necessary for the continued existence of Left Hand Path practitioners because some sort of law-based, conformist, state is to a degree necessary for human survival as far as the masses are concerned. There must be laws, regulations, and so forth for cultural stability. If one looks at society as a pyramid with the majority at the bottom and the few at the top, the lower you go on a sociological scale, the more the conformist mentality is to be expected. Moreover, this forms the basis of an orderly economy. Whereas with the Left Hand Path, where we find the individualistic dreamer and thinker or magician who is someone more at the top of this sociological pyramid and at the end of the spectrum which also has its role in the over all health of a society.

At one end of this spectrum is the absolutely free and enlightened individual; the other end is the absolutely bound and conforming collective of individuals. In the terminology of the Left Hand Path in the East they use the metaphor of the "bound" man and the "unbound" or liberated man. The ideal of the Eastern Left Hand Path is that of absolute freedom. The absolute freedom of the individual soul or psyche from enmeshment in the laws and regulations of this organism that is more vast than the individual soul or psyche.

In the Initiation of an individual we can see that the two Paths, and the two impulses, work in a way — or can work in a way — which is cooperative. They can work together almost like a single process. Here we are reminded of the alchemical principles of *Solve et Coagula*. You start with a coagulated state in which Initiates initially find themselves and this state needs to be transformed — so says the individual or so determines the individual — so they set out on a path of Initiation. This coagulated state must be dissolved. Initiates must separate, step back from the laws, rules, regulations which govern them, they must question them, they must question themselves and how they came to be the way they are and the laws and regulations which were imposed upon them at different times, consciously and unconsciously, and dissolve some of these bonds so that they can feel what it is to be independent in a free and fluid state, unbound by these rules and regulations and laws. They discover that changes can be caused to occur. But if they merely continue to exist inactively in this new state they find that no proving ground is provided for these changes. Therefore what is needed is that the initiate must reenter a state of being bound by the rules and regulations of human society, but now they interact in and within those laws in a new way, a way by which they retain knowledge gained from the Initiatory experience. There can occur a time in which there are periods of oscillation between these states of being bound, free of restraints, and then being once more bound to constraints. Herein lies a mystery of the *valknútr*.

This is something that when consciously applied in a magical and Initiatory way is a quite extraordinary, but it is analogous to things that everyone undergoes or should undergo in the process of simply growing up. For example, an infant is very much bound by laws and rules and regulations and is happily so bound. They like to stay in their little cribs, they drink their milk from their mothers, and just have very basic needs. But then they go through the so-called Terrible Twos where a kid loves to say "no" to everything, they learn how to refuse and say "no" and get great sense of independence of their beings from the way the higher forces, the adults in their lives, want them to do things. Then adolescence, of course, is a grander version of the same thing. So these periods of being unbound by laws and rules and regulations or laws upon the psyche are the times and psychic spaces — if you will — in which transformation takes place. That's when there is *separation*. The analysis of the rites of transformation by Arnold van Gennep indicates that people undergo rites of separation where they separate from the normal society then they transform in this special environment (of a lodge or woodland clearing or whatever the initiatory space is— a ritual chamber of some kind) and then they undergo rites of reintegration back into society, so that society as whole gains the benefits of the transformations that these people make in their lives. This is the way the process was intended to work. But in a world that is constantly assigning good and evil to every polarized contrasting pair attitudes such as, "Oh, rites of integration are good but rites of disintegration, of separation are bad, and certainly rites of transformation are bad because who are you to change, unless it is a change to make you even more conformist then you were before," are certain to arise.

Thus we see that sociological situations that formed some aspects of our culture led to misunderstandings of how these two poles of human activity, which we have conveniently characterized Right and Left Hand Path, actually function in a healthy integral and authentic society or culture.

IX
Antinomianism?

First of all we must define antinomianism. Those who are familiar with the contents of my book, *Lords of the Left-Hand Path* will be aware of antinomianism and its definition but not everyone is familiar with that book or with this concept. It literally means "against the lawism," *anti*, against, *nomian* is derived from the Greek νομος and has to do the law. So antinomianism is the practice of going against the grain if you will, going against the consensus norms as an exercise, or as a way of approaching a philosophy of life. Antinomianism is most pronounced in such movements we might characterize as "Satanic."

Originally this term was invented in the 16th century to discuss matters of Christian theology. Over the centuries, as is the case with many originally technical and context-specific terms, the use of the term was expanded to describe any and all situation in which individuals rebel against legal authority to exercise a higher good. Certainly Mircea Eliade used it to describe the practices of the Eastern *Vāmamārga*.

Examples of this principle are found where an entity is categorically, within the context of its own mythology, seen as a dissenter or a rebel. In the Hebraic mythology it is given the name *Satan* which literally merely means "the opponent," the one who stands against something else. So here we have the most perfect example of antinomianism in mythology in the sense that it is an entity and a principle which is set up to *oppose* something else. Originally in Hebrew myth Satan is the opponent of Man, the prosecuting attorney who accuses man before God. Satan and God can be seen to be on fairly friendly terms in the Book of Job, for example.

Now if someone determines at some point in life, or in the history of a culture, that in fact the *norm*, or the law-giver, is in fact evil or bad for and individual or culture to take up the cause of the rebel is not necessarily an evil thing *per se*. It is simply that you are taking up rebellion— a cosmic rebellion against the norm which has been determined to be bad after all.

We see that this principle is applied in different mythologies in different ways. For example, one might say it is an antinomian act when in Greek mythology Prometheus rebels against the orders of Zeus and brings the fire of enlightenment, or of consciousness, to mankind. Or when Óðinn kills his ancestor, the giant Ymir, and shapes the rational cosmos out of the parts of his body — a reflection of ancient Indo-European cosmogony — but there *was* a law, there was a *norm*, there was an organized form to the universe *before* the rebellion took place. It is just that a conscious entity in the form of Óðinn comes into being, evolves, looks around and says, "This world is bad, this world is not working properly. I'm going to rebel against its laws and overthrow this order." In other words go *against the law*, an act of antinomianism, "and establish a new law based upon a determination of what is good and right."

The United States of America was founded in an act of rebellion against divinely established norms. The Declaration of Independence was couched in the form of an indictment of the King of England who was incarnate the law — the absolute law — of his time. George III was an absolute monarch who ruled by divine right, yet he is brought up on charges of being a despot and a tyrant and in this way the rebellion is *justified*, but it is rebellion against the prevailing law nevertheless. For the most part in the world of 1776 the Founding Fathers — so avidly referred to as Bible-thumping, good Christian men by many in the American political Right of the past few decades — were in their own time actually commonly seen as the equivalent as devil-worshipers or Satanists. This consensus point of view is understandable in the cultural context of the day in the sense that the law, and the good, and the right was well known to the average conservative man to be that of absolute monarchy. Furthermore, it was well known that God wants men to be governed by monarchs — absolute monarchs — in a firm union of Church and State wherein the monarch is the Defender of the Faith and Head of the Church! So to rebel against George III was tantamount to rebellion against God. That was the clear and obvious consensus reality in the world of 1776. These men were committing acts of extreme antinomianism. So these things are not limited to religion or spiritual endeavors and it is true that the principle is widespread and we can see it at work in many ways historically.

Now we want to look at antinomianism specifically and discuss in some detail this idea as a key to personal development and ask whether it is necessary in such an endeavor. So let's look at the question of antinomianism in the practice of, for example, the Left Hand Path. We have already seen that the practice of the Left Hand Path in the Eastern world where the term was invented, the *Vāmamārga*, is a path of non-union. That is the individual self is not to be absorbed and meshed with the greater universe or god or universal consciousness, but rather it is to maintain its own individual, unique identity and does not unify with the whole. So it becomes a god-like entity in its own right— in other words it's a form of individual self-deification. In the Western monotheistic corollary the Left Hand Path becomes a rather crude God versus Satan paradigm.

When we look into the deeper background the idea of the Left Hand Path seems to have originally been related to ancient Indo-European ritual activity. The practitioner, the religious sacrificer, would face, for the most part, to the east — toward the rising sun — in performing rites. So that the south was on his right side and the north was on his left side so that the north becomes the *sinister* side. Note that this Latin word for "left" later took on negative connotations. The right hand goes to the equator the left to the pole, to the polestar, to the pole of the cosmos in the north. So here we have an equatorial, circular path denoted by the right hand and a polar path, a vertical polar path, indicated by the left hand as we stand facing east. Therefore the Left Hand Path denotes a vertical polar path and the Right Hand Path a circular equatorial pathway. And in the ancient idea of reincarnation for example that we have discussed elsewhere we saw that those are the two ways being indicated: the circular path being the way of the ancestors and rebirth within the clan, and the polar path being the divinization of the free individual person followed by possible reincarnation free of natural pathways. This latter type of individual has undergone a Left-Hand Path form of liberation of the soul from natural constraints.

So the question arises: is this antinomianism necessary to Initiatory development — especially when we look at it from a sort of Left Hand Path perspective or even an Odian perspective — is it *necessary*? Is it something which is essential to the practice of what it is we are talking about?

And the answers are — as one might expect — both yes and no.

Yes it is *often* necessary in certain cultural contexts for particular individuals. This is especially true in cultures corrupted by unreflective conformism. Antinomianism is often necessary because the culture and the environment, the spiritual environment, in which individual initiates find themselves is corrupted by this unreflective conformism and rebellion against cultural norms stemming from this conformism becomes necessary. This explains the necessity of a Declaration of Independence in a certain cultural context, or why a child raised as a Southern Baptist might gravitate toward Satanism in the journey of his initiation as a free man.

It is essentially a cultural or social construct that norms or laws are developed, and that people are expected to conform to them spiritually, physically, and in every other way. But when human beings live in such environments rebellions against norms are exercises in independent thought and may be in fact necessary to continued human development. If one, to give a very simple down-to-earth example, were brought up in a very unreflective fundamentalist religion of an unspiritual kind with just plenty of hellfire and brimstone, if that person were to wish to become an Initiate and actually explore a spiritual life in any kind of real way, *rebellion* would be necessary against the detrimental program to which that person had been subjected. In such an example an at least temporary embracing of

Satanism, paganism or other overt forms of rebellion would in fact probably be psychologically necessary for such a person in order to get a definite break with that old pattern of thought and programing.

This is akin to saying I want to tear this house down in order to rebuild something better. It is a reflection of the slaying of Ymir in order to create a new and better world. Historically we will find that it is in these repressive cultural environments that the Left Hand Path symbols with which we are most familiar such as Satan, Lucifer, Iblis and such things, that initially spring to mind in Western culture, emerge.

As far as antinomianism and its necessity is concerned, we find that it is not absolutely necessary. It is not necessary to go against the grain or rebel against the norms of your culture if in fact you live in a culture which promotes and facilitates the exercise of individuation, then no antinomianism is necessary.

Well where do we find these things?

We look at Óðinn and say he rebelled, and he created this new world — the one we live in now — endowed with the Runes and he is the chief god of the ancient Germanic peoples, so this is something where one might say, "Well here this figure of rebellion is the establishment." So in that culture that god's approach to the world was the highest form of its mythology, although it must be said that this way of approaching life was not the most *popular* way, it was certainly the highest form of the established method of exploring one's self and one's spiritual path. Therefore you would not rebel against Óðinn, that is one of the great mistakes or silly impulses in modern Odinism as it were. There is a general antinomian impulse in this Age of Satan as it is called, this Age of Rebellion, this Wolf Age we would call it in Germanic mythology, where everything is being turned on its head and things are in topsy-turvy kind of relation to one another. So what do people do with this impulse?

When they approach Germanic mythology, for example, they often start trying to "worship" Loki, which is quite annoying really. This is annoying because Loki is a *mythological figure* but not a *god* who was ever *worshipped* in any sort of cultic fashion in antiquity. Moreover, all of the things which these would-be Loki-worshipers are endeavoring to explore are all actually well established parts of the Odian environment and in fact many mythologists believe that Loki is just a sort of a *shadow side* of Óðinn himself. Loki only appears in Icelandic mythology and there is one example of the use of his name in English, but it was probably from a Scandinavian source also. So he is a mythological figure, but not an established *god* in the ancient pantheon who was worshiped in a cult or who received regular sacrifices or worship in the ancient north.

But that is not the point here, the point is that modern people when faced with this mythology and conditioned by an almost antinomian impulse, a rebellious impulse, which is abroad in our culture, gravitate towards these figures of rebellion against the norm or against the established order. But in the case, presented by Norse mythology, for example, such rebellion is unnecessary because the spiritual pathways and methods which the Initiate is seeking are perfectly well established things.

This also clarifies the discussion in in my book *Lords of the Left Hand Path*. I had to have criteria for what constitutes the Left Hand Path as an expression of spiritual rebellion, or dissent against the norms or against the established order. That was the criterion upon which the various people or ideas discussed were included, so that under those criteria the systematic treatment of Indo-European religions and the dark side aspects within it were excluded because such impulses perfectly well established and integrated into the whole system. There was no ongoing rebellion occurring in the spiritual lives of people, it was just another form of religion available to them.

Another strong contrast we might see in the same category is, for example, when one looks at Japanese culture especially at their indigenous native religion, the Way of the Gods, *Shinto*. There it is said that every person has a *kami* nature. *Kami* meaning "god," so that we understand that each persona has an inner god-nature, and people, individuals — through discipline and through devotion and concentration and through mastery of their crafts and other things — can fulfill or manifest their *kami*-nature in this life. Just like in India people, yogans, become gods incarnate and such things. In pagan Europe the deification of men, or at least their elevation to the status of divine heroes, was not uncommon at all; it was considered legitimate. Not ordinary but nevertheless a common enough thing. This impulse becomes corrupted, with the divination of emperors and such. But when the divinization of heroes is honestly and forthrightly used and practiced within a culture we see it is an expression of the idea that every individual has this sort of indwelling divine principle and it is the work of that individual, the best work of that individual, to unfold that nature within himself and become that thing. There is a book published just after the Second World War, and the title says it all really, *Shinto in Essence as Illustrated by the Faith in a Glorified Personality* by Genshe Kato. In this the author describes one man who was a nineteenth century soldier for whom a temple or shrine was built and he is considered to be a god. So there gods are being produced. There are sword makers and all kinds of people with special characteristics in Japan who are considered to be living gods in this way. So it is not uncommon. This book by Genshe Kato explains that this what is occurring: there is a divine principle and there are god-men and all people are this *in potentia*. But this is only achieved through action and effort, and through work and discipline and the expenditure of heroic effort which unfolds this spirit in individuals. Thus in the mythological understanding of people living in these cultures there are individuals who are thought to have unfolded this nature and become gods incarnate. But they are not rebelling against their culture, they are not embracing rebellious forms, tearing their norms down. No, this is at least part of the norm of their culture.

So in the healthiest forms of culture antinomianism is unnecessary, and if practiced it would actually be detrimental and bad. In a corrupt, bad society, in a society which is already corrupted and is really practicing bad cultural principles, then, of course, rebelling against it is necessary. So antinomianism is then necessary. We can boil this down, or scale this back, to the life of individuals. If you have been programmed by negative things, such as in our fundamentalist Christian example, then antinomianism is a tool or weapon in your arsenal for your own improvement, and for your spiritual reconstitution. But if the society or culture is actually supportive of spiritual quests and endeavors, if it is a *heroic* culture in other words, then rebelling against those norms would tend to be counter productive. I think that is pretty clear and we see historical examples of both here before us.

So if we go back to the example in the Eastern world, in India, and if we go back in time to the Vedic Age we will discover that there is really no "Left Hand Path" there. There are gods such as Varuna who are rather like dark gods somewhat analogous to Óðinn, and they are part of the pantheon also. Or we see that Shiva has many characteristics which are dark. Rudra has many of these same aspects but those gods and those figures are organic parts of a larger pantheon, as a *whole*. They are parts of a greater whole, and they belong to the over all order as it is. But as Hinduism and Buddhism historically start to develop in an increasingly world-rejecting direction those elements are shoveled to the side a little bit and at that point, and only at that point, does the technique or even the terminology of *Vāmamārga* emerge. At that point it becomes necessary for some practitioners to follow a path consciously *contrary* to the consensus norm. This is the beginning, or the root, of any conscious practice of antinomianism for the sake of spiritual development. By the way, this is the only kind of antinomianism we are addressing here. Merely going against the grain to be contrary is more akin to a personality disorder, or an artistic conceit, than it is to a spiritual path. But sadly it must be said that there is quite a number of people with that particular disorder who today masquerade as spiritual seekers.

www.ingramcontent.com/pod-product-compliance
Lightning Source LLC
Chambersburg PA
CBHW020959090426
42736CB00010B/1391